学·研·文·库

英国维多利亚时代名人诗歌

杜　平｜编译

中央编译出版社
CCTP Central Compilation & Translation Press

图书在版编目（CIP）数据

英国维多利亚时代名人诗歌 /杜平编译. —北京：
中央编译出版社，2019.9
ISBN 978-7-5117-3703-8

Ⅰ. ①英…
Ⅱ. ①杜…
Ⅲ. ①诗集—英国—近代
Ⅳ. ① I561.24

中国版本图书馆 CIP 数据核字（2018）第 300352 号

英国维多利亚时代名人诗歌

出 版 人：葛海彦
责任编辑：杜永明
责任印制：刘　慧
出版发行：中央编译出版社
地　　址：北京西城区车公庄大街乙 5 号鸿儒大厦 B 座（100044）
电　　话：（010）52612345（总编室）　（010）52612339（编辑室）
　　　　　（010）52612316（发行部）　（010）52612346（馆配部）
传　　真：（010）66515838
经　　销：全国新华书店
印　　刷：三河市华东印刷有限公司
开　　本：710 毫米 ×1000 毫米　1/16
字　　数：287 千字
印　　张：16.5
版　　次：2019 年 9 月第 1 版
印　　次：2019 年 9 月第 1 次印刷
定　　价：79.00 元

网　　址：www.cctphome.com　邮　　箱：cctp@cctphome.com
新浪微博：@中央编译出版社　微　　信：中央编译出版社(ID: cctphome)
淘宝店铺：中央编译出版社直销店(http://shop108367160.taobao.com)(010)55626985

本社常年法律顾问：北京市吴栾赵阎律师事务所律师　闫军　梁勤
凡有印装质量问题，本社负责调换，电话：（010）55626985

译者前言

英国维多利亚时代（1837—1901）的诗歌是19世纪前叶浪漫主义诗歌的延续和消退，虽说在成就及影响上远不及浪漫主义诗歌，但也涌现了像丁尼生、勃朗宁夫妇、罗塞蒂兄妹等一大批杰出的诗人。维多利亚时代是英国最为强盛的时期，大英帝国是名副其实的“日不落帝国”，势力几乎遍及全球各个角落。在这一背景下，英国文学也发生了一些深刻变化，诗歌已很难全方位反映这一时期动荡不安的时代特征和思想观念的巨变，小说成了这一时期主要的文学形式。就诗人而言，他们更多关注的是表现日益高涨的帝国意识、民主意识以及道德观念，因此个人主观感受和个人主义色彩在诗歌中有所淡化。但总体上看，一方面，这一时期的诗歌与浪漫主义诗歌有着千丝万缕的联系；另一方面，诗歌在主题、体裁、韵律等方面表现更为多元，也有所创新和突破。特别是在19世纪末到20世纪初的文化转型时期，维多利亚诗人所做的自觉探索为英语现代诗歌的发展奠定了基础。

诗歌翻译是一件苦差事，把它比作戴着脚镣跳舞一点不为过。翻译过程中有许多因素需要权衡，形式和内容的配合、诗意的表达、取与舍、译文中“度”的把握等都影响着译者。翻译过程中，常有言不逮意的感觉，故时常挣扎于言辞之间。译者是第一次系统尝试翻译诗歌，在翻译中主要采用了自由韵式，韵律方面考虑较少，似是一大遗憾，只好留待以后弥补。

本书选取了26位作家的诗作，共78首诗歌，其中有相当一部分未见正式译文。选译的诗歌主题与体裁范围较广，除选取了维多利亚时代重要诗人，亦选取了像狄更斯、萨克雷、梅瑞狄斯、爱略特和哈代等小说家创作的诗歌，基本上覆盖了那个时代的主要诗人。

鉴于译者水平有限，译文中必定有许多不妥之处，若有谬误出现，责任全在译者本人，敬请同仁和诗歌爱好者批评指正。

2018 年 7 月 25 日于华凤校区

目 录
CONTENTS

Alfred Lord Tennyson
阿尔弗雷德·丁尼生

阿尔弗雷德·丁尼生（Alfred Lord Tennyson, 1809—1892）的创作生涯跨越大半个世纪，前期作品多为抒情短诗，后期则以长篇叙事诗为主。丁尼生追求诗歌艺术的完美，其诗歌风格多样，辞藻华丽，韵律和谐，节奏明快。回忆与追思是丁尼生诗歌中两个最常见的主题。《食人莲》（*The Lotus-Eaters*, 1832）、《尤利西斯》（*Ulysses*, 1842）、长篇叙事诗《公主》（*Princess*, 1847）以及《悼念》（*In Memoriam*, 1850）等是他的代表性诗作。丁尼生的诗歌不但表现了维多利亚时代的社会生活和伦理道德，而且也继承和发扬了英国诗歌的伟大传统，无论就作品数量与质量而言，他都不愧是维多利亚时代最伟大的诗人。

All Things Will Die

Clearly the blue river chimes in its flowing
Under my eye;
Warmly and broadly the south winds are blowing
Over the sky;
One after another the white clouds are fleeting;
Every heart this May morning in joyance is beating
Full merrily;
Yet all things must die.

The stream will cease to flow;
The wind will cease to blow;
The clouds will cease to fleet;
The heart will cease to beat;
For all things must die.
All things must die.
Spring will come never more.
O, vanity!
Death waits at the door.
See! our friends are all forsaking
The wine and the merrymaking.
We are call'd—we must go.

万物皆会消亡

清澈湛蓝的河水欢快地流淌，
映入我的眼帘；
从南方吹入的暖风扑面而来，
掠过长空；
片片白云在天空疾驰；
五月的清晨心儿兴奋地跳动
充满喜悦；
然而万物皆会消亡。

溪流会停止流淌；
风儿会停止吹拂；
云彩会驻留天空；
心脏会停止跳动；
因万物必将消亡。
万物皆会消亡。
春天将不再来，
哦，多么虚妄！
死神滞留在门旁。
瞧啊！我们的挚友正在告别
醉生梦死，不再寻欢作乐。
召唤我们了——我们必须离去。

Laid low, very low,
In the dark we must lie.
The merry glees are still;
The voice of the bird
Shall no more be heard,
Nor the wind on the hill.
O, misery!
Hark! death is calling
While I speak to ye,
The jaw is falling,
The red cheek paling,
The strong limbs failing;
Ice with the warm blood mixing;
The eyeballs fixing.
Nine times goes the passing bell:
Ye merry souls, farewell.
The old earth
Had a birth,
As all men know,
Long ago.
And the old earth must die.
So let the warm winds range,
And the blue wave beat the shore;
For even and morn
Ye will never see
Thro' eternity.
All things were born.
Ye will come never more,
For all things must die.

躺下身子，越来越低，
我在黑暗中躺下。
喜悦与快乐经久不止；
鸟儿的啼声
再也听不见了，
山坡上的风儿也停了。
哦，多么痛苦！
听啊！死亡在召唤了，
我对你说话的当儿，
下颚开始低垂，
绯红的脸颊变得苍白；
强壮的四肢变得无力；
温暖的血液变得冰凉；
眼球不再转动。
远逝的钟声敲响了九次：
再见吧，欢乐的灵魂！
古老的土地
孕育了生命，
但是众人皆知，
那已年湮世远。
古老的土地必定衰亡。
因此，让那温暖的风狂吹，
让那蓝色的波涛猛击海岸；
不管是夜晚还是清晨
你将永远
看不透亘古不变的永生。
万物生生不息。
但你再也不能回来了，
万物皆会消亡。

The Deserted House

Life and Thought have gone away
Side by side,
Leaving door and windows wide:
Careless tenants they!
All within is dark as night:
In the windows is no light;
And no murmur at the door,
So frequent on its hinge before.
Close the door, the shutters close,
Or thro' the windows we shall see
The nakedness and vacancy
Of the dark deserted house.

Come away: no more of mirth
Is here or merry – making sound.
The house was builded of the earth,
And shall fall again to ground.

Come away: for Life and Thought
Here no longer dwell;

遗弃的房间

生命和思想已然离去
肩并肩，
留下大门和窗户洞开：
他们是多么粗心的房客！
房间内如暗夜一片漆黑
窗户内没有一丝光亮；
房门边没有嘈杂之声，
从前门上的铰链时常发出那种声音。
关上房门，关上百叶窗，
透过窗户，我们会看到
房内空无一物，
只有一间幽暗阴森、被遗弃的房间。

离去吧：再也没有了欢乐，
再也没有了快乐的声响。
泥土建成的房屋，
将垮塌重归泥土。

离去吧：因生命和思想
再也不在此栖息；

But in a city glorious—
A great and distant city—have bought
A mansion incorruptible.
Would they could have stay'd with us!

但在这个光荣的城市——
一个伟大而遥远的城市——已赎回
一座不朽的大厦。
但愿它们与我们同在!

Crossing the Bar

Sunset and evening star,
And one clear call for me!
And may there be no moaning of the bar,
When I put out to sea,

But such a tide as moving seems asleep,
Too full for sound and foam,
When that which drew from out the boundless deep
Turns again home.

Twilight and evening bell,
And after that the dark!
And may there be no sadness of farewell,
When I embark;

For though from out our bourne of Time and Place
The flood may bear me far,
I hope to see my Pilot face to face
When I have crost the bar.

渡沙洲

落日，晚星，
清朗之声将我召唤！
唯愿沙洲处不再悲鸣，
此时我将出海远航。

但涌动的潮汐似已沉睡，
吞没了浪花和潮声，
潮汐来自无边无际的大海深处
仍要转回到大海的家。

暮光降临，晚钟响起，
黑暗笼罩后，
唯愿诀别不再悲伤，
此时我将登船起航；

小溪穿越时空
聚成洪流，带我奔向远方，
我希望亲眼目睹我的领航人，
因为我已渡过沙洲。

Tears, Idle Tears

Tears, idle tears, I know not what they mean,
Tears from the depth of some divine despair
Rise in the heart, and gather to the eyes,
In looking on the happy Autumn-fields,
And thinking of the days that are no more.

Fresh as the first beam glittering on a sail,
That brings our friends up from the underworld,
Sad as the last which reddens over one
That sinks with all we love below the verge;
So sad, so fresh, the days that are no more.

Ah, sad and strange as in dark summer dawns
The earliest pipe of half-awakened birds
To dying ears, when unto dying eyes
The casement slowly grows a glimmering square;
So sad, so strange, the days that are no more.

Dear as remembered kisses after death,
And sweet as those by hopeless fancy feigned
On lips that are for others; deep as love,
Deep as first love, and wild with all regret;
O Death in Life, the days that are no more!

为什么流泪

泪水，无故的泪水，我不知为何流，
来自神圣的绝望的深处
在心头涌起，汇聚到我的双眼，
俯视秋天欢畅的田野，
想起那一去不复返的时光。

像闪烁在船帆上的第一缕阳光般清新，
把我们的挚友拯救出冥府，
像洒在船帆上的最后一抹夕阳般忧伤
带着我所爱的一切沉入天边；
如此忧伤，如此清新，时光一去不复返。

啊，悲伤、奇异如幽暗的夏日黎明，
半醒的鸟儿唱响了最早的一支曲子，
音乐飘进了临终者的耳朵，他的目光转向
窗扉透出的一团摇曳的亮光；
多么悲伤，多么神奇，时光一去不复返。

亲切如死后难以忘怀的亲吻，
甜蜜如幻想
假意挂在唇上慰藉他人；深沉如真爱，
深刻如初恋的记忆，更因悔恨而癫狂；
啊，生命中的死神，时光一去不复返。

Elizabeth Barrett Browning
伊丽莎白·巴瑞特·勃朗宁

伊丽莎白·巴瑞特·勃朗宁（Elizabeth Barrett Browning，1806—1861）是维多利亚时代最优秀的抒情女诗人之一。她出生在一个富有的家庭，自幼多病，身体孱弱，但接受过良好的教育。巴瑞特·勃朗宁少女时代便钟情于诗歌创作，十三岁时就出版了第一部诗集。三十九岁时她结识了罗伯特·勃朗宁（Robert Browning），由于受到她父亲的竭力阻挠，两人被迫远赴异国他乡，婚后长期生活在意大利，度过了余生。她最优秀的诗集《意大利十四行诗》（*Sonnet from the Portuguese*，1850）就是对他们炽烈的爱情的最好诠释；《奥罗拉·利》（*Aurora Leigh*，1857）是一部诗歌体裁的小说，也是对她的爱情故事的注脚。

Change Upon Change

Five months ago the stream did flow,
The lilies bloomed within the sedge,
And we were lingering to and fro,
Where none will track thee in this snow,
Along the stream, beside the hedge.
Ah, Sweet, be free to love and go!
For if I do not hear thy foot,
The frozen river is as mute,
The flowers have dried down to the root:
And why, since these be changed since May,
Shouldst thou change less than they.

And slow, slow as the winter snow
The tears have drifted to mine eyes;
And my poor cheeks, five months ago
Set blushing at thy praises so,
Put paleness on for a disguise.
Ah, Sweet, be free to praise and go!
For if my face is turned too pale,
It was thine oath that first did fail, —
It was thy love proved false and frail, —
And why, since these be changed enow,
Should I change less than thou.

变幻无穷

五个月前，小溪水潺潺流淌，
莎草四周百合花绽放，
我们曾在这儿流连忘返，
顺着小溪，围绕树篱。
雪地里无人寻觅你的踪迹，
啊，亲爱的，让我们尽情欢悦！
倘若我听不到你的脚步声，
世界便如冰封的河流一般哑寂，
花儿凋落回到树根：
为何五月尽逝，万千变化，
独你风采不减。

如冬雪缓慢飘落
我的双眼噙满泪花；
五个月前，我清瘦的脸颊
因你赞美而露出羞涩，
故带苍白的脸颊只为了掩饰。
啊，亲爱的，让我们尽情赞美，尽情欢愉！
假如我的脸色变得太苍白，
那也是因你当初山盟海誓沦为一场空，
你的爱虚情假意又脆弱，
唉！一切已物是人非，
但愿我还能比你光彩照人。

A Dead Rose

O Rose! who dares to name thee?
No longer roseate now, nor soft, nor sweet;
But pale, and hard, and dry, as stubble - wheat, —
Kept seven years in a drawer—thy titles shame thee.

The breeze that used to blow thee
Between the hedgerow thorns, and take away
An odour up the lane to last all day, —
If breathing now, —unsweetened would forego thee.

The sun that used to smite thee,
And mix his glory in thy gorgeous urn,
Till beam appeared to bloom, and flower to burn, —
If shining now, —with not a hue would light thee.

The dew that used to wet thee,
And, white first, grow incarnadined, because
It lay upon thee where the crimson was, —
If dropping now, —would darken where it met thee.

The fly that lit upon thee,
To stretch the tendrils of its tiny feet,
Along thy leaf 's pure edges, after heat, —

枯萎的玫瑰

哦，玫瑰！谁敢直呼汝名？
如今你不再红光焕发、不再娇柔和芬芳；
变得苍白、坚硬，似干枯的麦茬，
抽屉里弃置七年——你的芳名因此而蒙羞。

微风曾经吹拂你
透过树篱之间的荆棘
吹散了整日弥漫在小巷的香气，
如果现在吸口气，——淡淡的花香将因此而不再为你所有。

太阳曾经把你摧残，
把他的荣耀混合在你绚丽的瓮中，
直到阳光灿如繁花盛开，花红似火燃烧，
如果此刻艳阳高照，——一丝的色彩，也将因此而遁离你的左右。

露水曾经沾湿你的花叶，
起初白色的露水逐渐变为深红色，
因为它深卧于一片绯红之中，
如果露水此刻滴落，——它将因此而使你黯然失色。

栖息在你上面的苍蝇，
沿着你纯洁的叶子边缘，
伸展它纤细触角的卷须，一阵炙烤后，

If lighting now, —would coldly overrun thee.

The bee that once did suck thee,
And build thy perfumed ambers up his hive,
And swoon in thee for joy, till scarce alive, —
If passing now, —would blindly overlook thee.

The heart doth recognise thee,
Alone, alone! The heart doth smell thee sweet,
Doth view thee fair, doth judge thee most complete, —
Though seeing now those changes that disguise thee.

Yes, and the heart doth owe thee
More love, dead rose! than to such roses bold
As Julia wears at dances, smiling cold! —
Lie still upon this heart—which breaks below thee!

如果此时点燃，——你将被无情蹂躏。

蜜蜂曾经吸吮你的汁液，
把芳香的琥珀建在他的蜂巢上，
他兴奋地醉卧在你身上，直到奄奄一息，
如果他现在飞过，——会对你视若无睹。

只有心儿识得你，
哪怕孑然一身，我的心照样能闻出你的芳香，
照样能看清你的美，照样能鉴赏你的完美，
哪怕此时眼里的变化会掩饰你的真容。

是的，我的心欲把更多的爱献给你，
枯萎的玫瑰！而不献给茱莉亚舞会上戴的那些
夺人眼目的玫瑰，带着冷笑的玫瑰！
平静地躺卧在这颗心上——哪怕在你花下心儿碎！

Sonnet 14: If Thou Must Love Me, Let It Be for Nought

If thou must love me, let it be for nought
Except for love's sake only. Do not say
'I love her for her smile—her look—her way
Of speaking gently, —for a trick of thought
That falls in well with mine, and certes brought
A sense of pleasant ease on such a day'—
For these things in themselves, Beloved, may
Be changed, or change for thee, —and love, so wrought,
May be unwrought so. Neither love me for
Thine own dear pity's wiping my cheeks dry, —
A creature might forget to weep, who bore
Thy comfort long, and lose thy love thereby!
But love me for love's sake, that evermore
Thou mayst love on, through love's eternity.

十四行诗第十四首：如果你爱我，那就该别无他求

如果你爱我，那就该别无他求！
以爱的理由而独爱我。不要说
“我爱她的微笑、爱她的容颜——
爱她低语时温婉的仪态——因那爱意
恰合了我的心意，那一天，
自会带来无比愉悦的舒畅。”
但是，亲爱的，这些事物本身
不可能恒久不变，即或是因你也会生变，
令人心动的爱也会变得悄无声息。
爱我，就不要拿你珍贵的怜惜来揩干我的脸颊，
一个人也许会忘掉哭泣，因为
长久深怀你的慰藉，终会因此失去你的爱！
但是请你以爱的名义爱我，唯独如此
你的爱才能延续，直至不朽。

Robert Browning
罗伯特·勃朗宁

罗伯特·勃朗宁（Robert Browning，1812—1889）出生在伦敦一个富商之家，年少时期接受了良好的教育，加之他曾到俄国和意大利等国的旅行经历，为他后来的诗歌创作提供了丰富的素材。勃朗宁曾专门从事过一段时间的诗剧写作，虽然并不十分成功，但是这段经历对他的戏剧独白手法在诗歌中的应用起到了关键作用，因而也对后来的英国文学产生了深远影响。罗伯特·勃朗宁与伊丽莎白·巴瑞特相识相爱，在意大利生活的时光是他们夫妇诗歌创作的黄金时期。罗伯特·勃朗宁的诗歌语言生动、节奏鲜明、通俗易懂，广受世界各国读者喜爱，例如，《我的已故的公爵夫人》（*My Last Duchess*，1842）、《异国思乡情》（*Home - Thoughts from Abroad*，1845）等诗篇至今流传不衰。

Home – Thoughts from Abroad

Oh, to be in England
Now that April's there,
And whoever wakes in England
Sees, some morning, unaware,
That the lowest boughs and the brushwood sheaf
Round the elm – tree bole are in tiny leaf,
While the chaffinch sings on the orchard bough
In England—now!

And after April, when May follows,
And the whitethroat builds, and all the swallows!
Hark, where my blossomed pear – tree in the hedge
Leans to the field and scatters on the clover
Blossoms and dewdrops—at the bent spray's edge—
That's the wise thrush; he sings each song twice over,
Lest you should think he never could recapture
The first fine careless rapture!
And though the fields look rough with hoary dew,
All will be gay when noontide wakes anew
The buttercups, the little children's dower
—Far brighter than this gaudy melon – flower!

异国思乡情

啊，梦回英格兰
适逢四月天，
英伦早起人
无意间均可见
低垂的大树枝和灌木丛
围绕榆树枝干，正吐出嫩叶，
果园树枝上的燕雀在欢唱
此时——身处英格兰该多美妙！

四月逝去，五月来临，
白喉莺和燕子正把巢来筑！
听！树篱里鲜花绽放的梨树
紧挨田野，花瓣和露珠
洒落在三叶草上——在荒草地的小树枝边缘
有一只聪明的画眉鸟；他在反复吟唱，
唯恐你认为他不会去重温
第一回无忧无虑的欢畅！
白色露水使田野凌乱不堪，
但白昼醒来时，万物将欢悦，
金凤花，还有孩子们的嫁妆
——比俗气的香瓜花更绚丽！

Meeting at Night

I

The grey sea and the long black land;
And the yellow half – moon large and low;
And the startled little waves that leap
In fiery ringlets from their sleep,
As I gain the cove with pushing prow,
And quench its speed i' the slushy sand.

II

Then a mile of warm sea – scented beach;
Three fields to cross till a farm appears;
A tap at the pane, the quick sharp scratch
And blue spurt of a lighted match,
And a voice less loud, thro' its joys and fears,
Than the two hearts beating each to each!

相约夜色下

一

灰色的大海，绵延幽暗的陆地；
阔大的黄色半月低垂天空；
惊醒的细浪从睡梦里跃起，
溅起串串闪烁的小水波，
小舟劈波斩浪驶入海湾，
突然停歇在泥沙地里。

二

沙滩上弥漫着暖和的海腥味；
穿过三块田地，才见得一家农场，
轻叩窗户，传出急促而尖利的擦刮声，
点燃的火柴迸发出一团蓝光，
又喜又怕，两颗相对的心怦怦狂跳，
声音盖过了喃喃细语。

Life in a Love

Escape me?
Never—
Beloved!
While I am I, and you are you,
So long as the world contains us both,
Me the loving and you the loth
While the one eludes, must the other pursue.
My life is a fault at last, I fear:
It seems too much like a fate, indeed!
Though I do my best I shall scarce succeed.
But what if I fail of my purpose here?
It is but to keep the nerves at strain,
To dry one's eyes and laugh at a fall,
And, baffled, get up and begin again, —
So the chace takes up one's life, that's all.
While, look but once from your farthest bound
At me so deep in the dust and dark,
No sooner the old hope goes to ground
Than a new one, straight to the self-same mark,
I shape me—
Ever
Removed!

生死相依

离我而去？
你绝不会——
亲爱的！
我是我，你是你，
只要世界容得下我俩，
我一心爱恋你，你却不情愿，
只要一方逃避，另一方必穷追不舍。
恐怕，我的人生终究是一场过错：
真的，仿佛命运在作弄！
尽管千般努力，却罕有成功。
但即便不达目的，又该如何？
那只不过是神经紧绷，
擦干眼泪，笑对失落，
迷惘过后，站起身来重新开始，
耗尽毕生追逐你，不过如此而已！
然而仅此一次从你最遥远的尽头
凝视深处尘世和黑暗中的我，
一当旧的希望化为尘土
新的希望便应运而生，初衷不改
我形我塑——
永远不变
纵使天各一方！

One Way of Love

I

All June I bound the rose in sheaves.
Now, rose by rose, I strip the leaves
And strew them where Pauline may pass.
She will not turn aside? Alas!
Let them lie. Suppose they die
The chance was they might take her eye.

II

How many a month I strove to suit
These stubborn fingers to the lute!
To – day I venture all I know.
She will not hear my music? So!
Break the string; fold music's wing:
Suppose Pauline had bade me sing!

III

My whole life long I learned to love.
This hour my utmost art I prove
And speak my passion—heaven or hell?
She will not give me heaven? 'Tis well!
Lose who may—I still can say,
Those who win heaven, blest are they!

恋爱方式

一
整个六月我扎好一束束玫瑰花
而现在，我亲手剥掉一朵朵花叶，
把它们撒在波琳会经过的地方
她会视若无睹？唉！
让花蕾躺卧在那里吧。假如它们枯萎了
它们或许能够吸引她的目光。

二
多少个月我勤勉学艺
用我那僵硬的手指抚弄琴弦！
今天我要敞开心扉告诉她一切。
她却不愿听我的曲子？唉！
琴弦断了，音乐之翼折了：
假如波琳恳求我唱一首歌该多好！

三
我耗尽毕生学着去爱。
此时该我证实卓越的艺术才华了，
该我倾诉衷肠了——是天堂或是地狱？
她不会给我天堂？——那也无妨！
我仍旧要说，输赢无常，
祝福那些走进天堂的人们！

Matthew Arnold
马修·阿诺德

马修·阿诺德（Matthew Arnold, 1822—1888）是维多利亚时代最著名的批评家和诗人之一，被称作那个时代新文化的倡导者。阿诺德曾任牛津大学诗学教授（1857—1867）。他主张诗歌本身就是对生活的批评，要反映时代的要求，需有追求道德和智力“解放”的精神。其诗歌和评论对时弊很敏感，并能作出理性的评判。阿诺德的诗歌语言简朴，追求一种结构上的对称。但他的诗歌也流露出一种 19 世纪浪漫主义的悲观情绪，表达了维多利亚时代宗教与科学冲突带来的社会信仰危机。这一主题在他最著名的诗篇《多佛海滩》（*Dover Beach*，1851）中得到了充分表达。阿诺德的主要代表作有《多佛海滩》（*Dover Beach*，1851）、《郡莱布和罗斯托》（*Sohrab and Rustum*，1853）、《吉卜赛学者》（*The Scholar Gipsy*，1853）以及《文化与无政府主义》（*Culture and Anarchy*，1869）等。

Youth's Agitations

When I shall be divorced, some ten years hence,
From this poor present self which I am now;
When youth has done its tedious vain expense
of passions that for ever ebb and flow;

Shall I not joy youth's heats are left behind,
And breathe more happy in an even clime—
Ah no, for then I shall begin to find
A thousand virtues in this hated time!

Then I shall wish its agitations back,
And all its thwarting currents of desire;
Then I shall praise the heat which then I lack,
And call this hurrying fever, generous fire;

And sigh that one thing only has been lent
To youth and age in common—discontent.

青春的激情

大约十年后，我将离去，
因我现在已是风烛残年，
当青春已经耗尽，
热情一如海潮进退消长；

难道我不喜欢留住青春的热度？
不愿意在平和的空气里快乐呼吸？
啊！绝非如此，为往昔，我要开始去找寻
这个令人痛恨的时代里的千百种美好德行！

我愿青春的激情回到身边，
唤回我那被压抑的欲望涌流；
我要赞美离我远去的热情，
呼唤这急促的狂热，慷慨的烈焰；

感叹我们唯一共同的拥有
已献给了青年和老年——生不逢时。

Growing Old

What is it to grow old?
Is it to lose the glory of the form,
The lustre of the eye?
Is it for beauty to forego her wreath?
Yes, but not for this alone.

Is it to feel our strength—
Not our bloom only, but our strength—decay?
Is it to feel each limb
Grow stiffer, every function less exact,
Each nerve more weakly strung?

Yes, this, and more! but not,
Ah, 'tis not what in youth we dreamed 'twould be!
'Tis not to have our life
Mellowed and softened as with sunset-glow,
A golden day's decline!

变老

变老意味着什么?
是失掉身形的光彩,
双眼的光泽?
是美丽的容颜不再有花环?
是的,但又不仅如此。

是感到身体的力量
不再旺盛,而且开始衰减?
是感觉每一肢体
变得僵硬,功能失之精准,
每一根神经不再紧绷?

是的,比之更甚,但又非全是,
啊,它并非青年时期所梦想的东西!
它不是把生活
变得像落日余晖般轻柔与温和,
黄金岁月已然消退!

'Tis not to see the world
As from a height, with rapt prophetic eyes,
And heart profoundly stirred;
And weep, and feel the fulness of the past,
The years that are no more!

It is to spend long days
And not once feel that we were ever young.
It is to add, immured
In the hot prison of the present, month
To month with weary pain.

It is to suffer this,
And feel but half, and feebly, what we feel:
Deep in our hidden heart
Festers the dull remembrance of a change,
But no emotion—none.

It is—last stage of all—
When we are frozen up within, and quite
The phantom of ourselves,
To hear the world applaud the hollow ghost
Which blamed the living man.

它不是带着预言家全神贯注的眼睛
登高看世界，
也不是内心深处的骚动；
哭泣之中感受以往的充实，
这样的年华已不再！

是度过绵长的岁月
而无时无刻不感怀曾经的风华正茂。
是阅历的增长，
是把今天囚禁于火热的牢房
是月复一月去经受衰老的痛楚。

是忍受这样的苦痛，
是我们感到身体羸弱，一半被掏空：
是我们深藏内心的感受
令迟钝而改变的记忆饱受煎熬，
但却全无感觉——一点没有。

老年是人生最后的梯级——
自身完全封冻
活在幻影中，
聆听世界为虚空的魑魅魍魉鼓掌，
而鬼神则在责难活着的人。

Requiescat

Strew on her roses, roses,
And never a spray of yew!
In quiet she reposes;
Ah, would that I did too!

Her mirth the world required;
She bathed it in smiles of glee.
But her heart was tired, tired,
And now they let her be.

Her life was turning, turning,
In mazes of heat and sound.
But for peace her soul was yearning,
And now peace laps her round.

Her cabined, ample spirit,
It fluttered and failed for breath.
Tonight it doth inherit
The vasty hall of death.

安魂曲

她身上撒满玫瑰，
没有一根紫杉小枝！
静静的，她安眠于此；
啊，但愿我亦长眠于此！

世界曾经离不开她的欢笑；
她沐浴在欢乐的笑声中。
但是，她已心力憔悴，厌倦了尘世，
现在就让她安息吧。

她的人生变幻无常，
转动于狂热与喧嚣的迷宫之中。
但她的内心却渴望安宁，
此时安宁终将她揽入怀中。

她的灵魂充溢，却被囚于身，
扑打着翅膀，已气息奄奄。
今夜她的灵魂终于找到了寓所
——宏大的死亡殿堂。

George Meredith
乔治·梅瑞狄斯

乔治·梅瑞狄斯（George Meredith，1828—1909）是小说家和诗人。他早年丧母，在寄宿学校度过了童年，后又在德国就读两年。在英国文学史上，梅瑞狄斯的主要成就表现在小说创作方面，如最为人知的作品《利己主义者》（*The Egoist*，1879）。他最有代表性的诗作是《现代爱情》（*Modern Love*，1862）和《大地欢歌》（*Poems and Lyrics of the Joy of Earth*，1883）。梅瑞狄斯的诗歌较为关注维多利亚时代人们的真实思想风貌和言谈举止，但由于其创作思想深奥，语言结构复杂，他的大多数作品只为少数文艺界精英所欣赏。

Dirge in Woods

A wind sways the pines,
And below
Not a breath of wild air;
Still as the mosses that glow
On the flooring and over the lines
Of the roots here and there.
The pine - tree drops its dead;
They are quiet, as under the sea.
Overhead, overhead
Rushes life in a race,
As the clouds the clouds chase;
And we go,
And we drop like the fruits of the tree,
Even we,
Even so.

森林挽歌

松树在风中摇曳，
树下
没有一丝气息扰动；
青苔发出微光，
静静地铺在地面，
洒在盘根错节的树根枝条上。
松果掉落下来；
静静地，仿佛沉入大海。
松树顶端，我们的头顶上，
生活如同竞技场上的一场追逐，
又似流云奔涌，你追我赶；
我们走了，
像树上的果实一样坠落，
人生无常，
概莫如斯。

One Twilight Hour

We saw the swallows gathering in the sky,
And in the osier – isle we heard them noise.
We had not to look back on summer joys,
Or forward to a summer of bright dye:
But in the largeness of the evening earth
Our spirits grew as we went side by side.
The hour became her husband and my bride.
Love that had robbed us so, thus blessed our dearth!
The pilgrims of the year waxed very loud
In multitudinous chatterings, as the flood
Full brown came from the West, and like pale blood
Expanded to the upper crimson cloud.
Love that had robbed us of immortal things,
This little moment mercifully gave,
Where I have seen across the twilight wave
The swan sail with her young beneath her wings.

暮色时光

看见燕子在天空结队飞行
听见它们在柳树小岛上叽叽喳喳。
不必回首夏日的快乐，
或者期盼夏日绚丽的色调：
但广袤的大地正沉入夜色中
肩并肩，我们兴致勃勃。
时光成了她的新郎，我的新娘。
爱情让我们一无所有，我们却因此而庆幸！
朝圣的人们在那儿喧哗不已，
周围已是人声鼎沸，
就像滔滔洪水由西滚滚而来，
又像淡淡的血液，升腾到绯红的云端。
爱窃掠了一切不朽之物，
但也悲悯地赐予我片刻欣慰，
透过黄昏的波光我又看见
一只天鹅护着羽翼下的幼鸟飞过长空。

Song (Untitled #2)

The moon is alone in the sky
As thou in my soul;
The sea takes her image to lie
Where the white ripples roll
All night in a dream,
With the light of her beam,
Hushedly, mournfully, mistily up to the shore.
The pebbles speak low
In the ebb and the flow,
As I when thy voice came at intervals, tuned to adore:
Nought other stirred
Save my heart all unheard
Beating to bliss that is past evermore.

歌（无题 2）

一轮孤月当空
犹如你进入我灵魂中；
大海带走她的影像
长卧于白浪翻滚的地方。
长夜沉入梦中，
带着她微笑的光芒，
静谧，哀伤，缥缈涌上海岸。
海滩上卵石低语
但听潮涨潮落，
当我调入爱慕之音，不时传来你的声音：
一切都不再涌动，
万籁寂静之中，唯有我心儿欣喜狂跳，
多少往事已成云烟。

Dante Gabriel Rossetti
但丁·加百列·罗塞蒂

但丁·加百列·罗塞蒂（Dante Gabriel Rossetti，1828—1882）出生在伦敦，是克里斯蒂娜·罗塞蒂的哥哥。他青年时代热衷于绘画，后又迷上诗歌创作。1848年，与一群志同道合的画家和作家一道，罗塞蒂成立了“先拉斐尔派兄弟会”（Pre – Raphaelite Brotherhood），成为这一艺术流派的创始人。该派别反对传统的经院派艺术，倡导振兴文艺复兴之前简洁和朴素的艺术风格。罗塞蒂的诗歌深受约翰·济慈（John Keats）的影响，注重突出诗歌语言美感和色彩，诗中有画，画中有诗是他诗歌创作的明显特征。他的大多诗歌语言优美、风格典雅，具有强烈的音乐效果，《女神》（*The Blessed Damozel*，1850）和《我妹妹的睡梦》（*My Sister's Sleep*，1850）是他最为后世称道的两部作品。

Autumn Song

Know'st thou not at the fall of the leaf
How the heart feels a languid grief
Laid on it for a covering,
And how sleep seems a goodly thing
In Autumn at the fall of the leaf?

And how the swift beat of the brain
Falters because it is in vain,
In Autumn at the fall of the leaf
Knowest thou not? and how the chief
Of joys seems—not to suffer pain?

Know'st thou not at the fall of the leaf
How the soul feels like a dried sheaf
Bound up at length for harvesting,
And how death seems a comely thing
In Autumn at the fall of the leaf?

秋歌

认识你无须待到秋叶落
何以心儿倦怠悲伤
还故作掩饰，
何以安睡似乐事
适逢秋来叶落时？

何以才思敏捷变迟缓
皆因所为成枉然，
适逢秋来叶儿落
孰能不识你？何以快乐之主
似不忍痛苦煎熬？

认识你无须待到秋叶落
何以心儿感觉似干草
捆扎终待收获来，
何以死亡似美事
适逢秋来叶落时？

First Love Remembered

Peace in her chamber, wheresoe'er
It be, a holy place:
The thought still brings my soul such grace
As morning meadows wear.
Whether it still be small and light,
A maid's who dreams alone,
As from her orchard – gate the moon
Its ceiling showed at night:
Or whether, in a shadow dense
As nuptial hymns invoke,
Innocent maidenhood awoke
To married innocence:
There still the thanks unheard await
The unconscious gift bequeathed:
For there my soul this hour has breathed
An air inviolate.

初次相爱的记忆

她的卧室平静又安宁，无论何处
都是一个圣洁的地方：
每当我想起，心灵倍感润泽，
仿佛清晨草地沾满雨露。
无论这恩泽何其渺小与轻贱，
它出自孤独寻梦少女的馈赠，
正如从她的果园大门，
月亮在夜晚才会显露它的顶点：
无论在多么幽深的阴影里，
当婚礼上的赞美诗唱响，
纯真的少女时代才会让人领悟到
婚后的清白：
还有多少未曾听闻的感激在期待
毫无自知遗赠的礼物：
我的灵魂此刻已呼吸到
一丝没有被玷污的空气。

Sonnet Lxxvii: Soul's Beauty

Under the arch of Life, where love and death,
Terror and mystery, guard her shrine, I saw
Beauty enthroned; and though her gaze struck awe,
I drew it in as simply as my breath.
Hers are the eyes which, over and beneath,
The sky and sea bend on thee, —which can draw,
By sea or sky or woman, to one law,
The allotted bondman of her palm and wreath.
This is that Lady Beauty, in whose praise
Thy voice and hand shake still, —long known to thee
By flying hair and fluttering hem, —the beat
Following her daily of thy heart and feet,
How passionately and irretrievably,
In what fond flight, how many ways and days!

十四行诗第二十七首：灵魂之美

生命的拱门下方，矗立着爱情与死亡，
恐怖与神秘，把守着她的神龛，我看见
美正在加冕即位；虽然她的凝视令人敬畏，
但我尽情汲取她的美，仿佛自如呼吸空气。
她的美是她的双眸，你无论走到天涯海角，
她都会把你注视，——迷恋大海、天空或者女人之美的人
都会遵从一个法则，
沦为她分派的奴隶，落入她的掌心和花环。
这就是那位美丽女士，她的赞美
让你的嗓音和双手还在颤抖，——她早已为你深悉，
你熟悉她飘逸的长发，熟悉她舞动的裙褶，
用你心跳和步伐追逐她每日的节拍，
你满怀激情、义无反顾，
一往情深、多方百计、不舍昼夜地寻觅她的踪迹！

Christina Rossetti
克里斯蒂娜·罗塞蒂

克里斯蒂娜·古奥尔吉娜·罗塞蒂（Christina Georgia Rossetti, 1830—1894）自幼研习古典文学、小说及神话故事，有着深厚的文学素养。她十二岁时开始文学创作，十八岁时便出版了第一部诗集。1862年出版了她最有名的诗集《魔鬼集市与其他诗歌》（*Goblin Market and Other Poems*, 1862），赢得了广泛关注，被誉为她所处时代最伟大的女诗人之一。罗塞蒂的诗歌大多短小精干，哲理丰富，充满睿智，至今仍为广大读者推崇。

Up – hill

Does the road wind uphill all the way?
Yes, to the very end.
Will the day's journey take the whole long day?
From morn to night, my friend.

But is there for the night a resting – place?
A roof for when the slow, dark hours begin.
May not the darkness hide it from my face?
You cannot miss that inn.

Shall I meet other wayfarers at night?
Those who have gone before.
Then must I knock, or call when just in sight?
They will not keep you waiting at that door.

Shall I find comfort, travel – sore and weak?
Of labour you shall find the sum.
Will there be beds for me and all who seek?
Yea, beds for all who come.

上山

上山的道路一直蜿蜒崎岖？
是的，一直到尽头。
今天旅途要整整一天？
从清晨到夜晚，我的朋友。

但夜晚有歇息的地方？
夜色慢慢来临时，会找到房间过夜，
黑夜会不会遮蔽它，让我找不到？
你不会错过那家客栈。

夜晚会碰见其他行人？
你会见到那些走在前面的旅人。
看见他们，要敲门叫醒他们？
他们不会让你在门外等候。

能找到舒适以解旅行之痛和劳累？
只要你付出艰辛就会找到。
有床位容纳我与所有找店住的人？
有的，凡来者人人有床位。

The First Day

I wish I could remember the first day,
First hour, first moment of your meeting me;
If bright or dim the season, it might be
Summer or winter for aught I can say.
So unrecorded did it slip away,
So blind was I to see and to foresee,
So dull to mark the budding of my tree
That would not blossom yet for many a May.
If only I could recollect it! Such
A day of days! I let it come and go
As traceless as a thaw of bygone snow.
It seemed to mean so little, meant so much!
If only now I could recall that touch,
First touch of hand in hand! —Did one but know!

第一天

但愿我能记住第一天，
与你初次相遇的每时每刻；
是明亮或阴暗的季节
是夏天还是冬天，我也说不清。
岁月无痕，悄悄溜走，
昏花的双眼已失先知先见，
愚钝之极在树上刻记发出的新芽
有多少个五月没有开花。
能记起那一刻该多好！
不平凡的一天啊！我却让它来了又消逝
似残雪消融，无影无踪。
看似微不足道，却意味深长
但愿我能回想起那一次触碰，
牵手的第一感觉！——唯我独知！

Remember

Remember me when I am gone away,
Gone far away into the silent land;
When you can no more hold me by the hand,
Nor I half turn to go yet turning stay.
Remember me when no more day by day
You tell me of our future that you plann'd:
Only remember me; you understand
It will be late to counsel then or pray.
Yet if you should forget me for a while
And afterwards remember, do not grieve:
For if the darkness and corruption leave
A vestige of the thoughts that once I had,
Better by far you should forget and smile
Than that you should remember and be sad.

记忆

记住我吧，我要离去了，
去到远方那片安静的土地；
到时你再也不能紧握我的手，
我也不会欲走还留。
记住我吧，当你再不能每日
向我讲述你描绘的前程锦绣：
只要记住我；你便懂得
劝告或央求为时已晚。
然而假如你要短暂地忘掉我
然后再记起我，也不要悲伤：
因为如果黑暗与堕落能留下
我曾经有过的思念的痕迹，
你不妨忘记和微笑，
且毋须因记起我而伤感。

De Profundis

Oh why is heaven built so far,
Oh why is earth set so remote?
I cannot reach the nearest star
That hangs afloat.

I would not care to reach the moon,
One round monotonous of change;
Yet even she repeats her tune
Beyond my range.

I never watch the scatter'd fire
Of stars, or sun's far-trailing train,
But all my heart is one desire,
And all in vain:

For I am bound with fleshly bands,
Joy, beauty, lie beyond my scope;
I strain my heart, I stretch my hands,
And catch at hope.

出自深处

哦，为何天堂要修得如此渺远，
哦，为何大地离天堂那么遥迢？
离我最近的那颗星，我也够不上，
它高悬天际。

我不在乎能否够到月亮，
那不过是一个变化单调的圆球；
甚至她一遍遍重复的曲调
也非我所及。

我从来不会遥望群星璀璨，
也不会仰望太阳拖着的烈焰，
然而我心无旁骛，
因所有欲望均徒劳无益。

我囿于肉身束缚，
欢乐和美丽超出我心之所及；
只有强压内心欲望，伸手向天，
捕获希望。

William Morris
威廉姆·莫里斯

威廉姆·莫里斯（William Morris，1834—1896）长期以来被称作维多利亚时代的伟人之一，是英国19世纪最著名的设计师，同时也是一名诗人、小说家、社会主义活动家。他的诗歌作品主要包括《桂妮薇儿的辩解及其他诗》（*The Defence of Guenevere and Other Poems*，1858）、《伊阿宋的生与死》（*The Life and Death of Jason*，1867）。

Love Is Enough

Love is enough: though the World be a-waning,
And the woods have no voice but the voice of complaining,
Though the sky be too dark for dim eyes to discover
The gold-cups and daisies fair blooming thereunder,
Though the hills be held shadows, and the sea a dark wonder,
And this day draw a veil over all deeds pass'd over,
Yet their hands shall not tremble, their feet shall not falter;
The void shall not weary, the fear shall not alter
These lips and these eyes of the loved and the lover.

爱就是知足

爱就足矣：即使世界日渐衰微，
森林无声，唯有哀怨之声升起，
即使天空暗淡，模糊的双眼难以远望，
但天际下，驴蹄草和邹菊仍争妍斗奇，
即使阴影遮蔽群山，大海幽暗成谜，
时光如面纱淹没了所有陈年旧事，
但他们的双手不会颤抖，脚步不会踯躅；
空虚不会令人疲倦，畏惧不能改变
相爱之人的亲吻和凝视。

Near But Far Away

She wavered, stopped and turned, methought her eyes,
The deep grey windows of her heart, were wet,
Methought they softened with a new regret
To note in mine unspoken miseries,
And as a prayer from out my heart did rise
And struggled on my lips in shame's strong net,
She stayed me, and cried "Brother!" our lips met,
Her deawr hands drew me into Paradise.
Sweet seemed that kiss till thence her feet were gone,
Sweet seemed the word she spake, while it might be
As wordless music—But truth fell on me,
And kiss and word I knew, and, left alone,
Face to face seemed I to a wall of stone,
While at my back there beat a boundless sea.

若即若离

她彷徨，停顿，转身四顾，我想她的双眼
——她心灵深处深灰色的窗扉，已泪光盈盈，
我想，新添的一丝悔意已使它们变得柔和
更在我心中记下了无言的痛苦，
当我心中升起祈望
却因羞愧坚韧的织网而难以启齿。
她拦住我，大声喊：“兄弟！”我们深情相吻，
她亲切的手把我拉进了天堂。
我们甜蜜相吻直到她的脚步从此消失，
她的话语甜蜜而温馨，
宛如无言的乐声——但此刻真相落到我头上，
我才懂得亲吻和她的话语，尽管我依旧孤单，
仿佛直面一堵石墙，
此时我身后，无边的大海拍击着海岸。

Verses for Pictures

Day.

I am Day; I bring again
Life and glory, Love and pain:
Awake, arise! from death to death
Through me the World's tale quickeneth.

Spring.

Spring am I, too soft of heart
Much to speak ere I depart:
Ask the Summer – tide to prove
The abundance of my love.

Summer.

Summer looked for long am I;
Much shall change or e' er I die.
Prithee take it not amiss
Though I weary thee with bliss.

时光画语

昼
我是白昼；我又带来
生命与荣光，爱意与痛苦：
醒来，起床！从死亡到死亡
穿越白昼，尘世间的传说生生不息。

春
春天是我，有一副温婉的心肠
离开前，道不尽千言万语：
请夏季作证
我的爱是何等丰厚。

夏
我是盼望已久的夏天；
纵使变化万千或我将永远消失。
请不要把它看作我的缺陷
哪怕因我狂喜而令你身心交瘁。

Autumn.

Laden Autumn here I stand
Worn of heart, and weak of hand:
Nought but rest seems good to me,
Speak the word that sets me free.

Winter.

I am Winter, that do keep
Longing safe amidst of sleep:
Who shall say if I were dead
What should be remembered?

Night.

I am Night: I bring again
Hope of pleasure, rest from pain:
Thoughts unsaid 'twixt Life and Death
My fruitful silence quickeneth.

秋

我站在硕果累累的秋天里
心儿憔悴，手已无力：
似乎只有安息才合我意，
吩咐下去，让我解脱吧。

冬

我是冬天，心里一直
渴望安然无恙进入冬眠：
假如我死去，谁会说
该记住什么？

夜

我是黑夜：我又带来
快乐的希望，痛苦的解脱：
生与死之间还有多少未言说的思考
宁静的夜不久将结出硕果。

Algernon Charles Swinburne
阿尔杰农·查尔斯·史文朋

阿尔杰农·查尔斯·史文朋（Algernon Charles Swinburne，1837—1909）出生于一个贵族家庭，从小受到良好的教育，先是在伊顿公学就读，后又进入牛津大学。他的文学生涯始于古典诗剧创作，如《罗莎蒙德》（*Rosamond*，1860）以及《阿塔兰塔在加里登》（*Atalanta in Calydon*，1865）都取得了较大成功，然而其主要成就还是在抒情诗歌创作方面。史文朋蔑视维多利亚时代的清规戒律和宗教教义，主张个人的审美享受和灵感抒发。他的诗歌多以大自然、爱情、死亡为题材，追求诗歌的音乐效果，注重节奏和韵律对主题的表现作用。

Love at Sea

WE ARE in love's land to - day;
Where shall we go?
Love, shall we start or stay,
Or sail or row?
There's many a wind and way,
And never a May but May;
We are in love's hand to - day;
Where shall we go?

Our landwind is the breath
Of sorrows kissed to death
And joys that were;
Our ballast is a rose;
Our way lies where God knows
And love knows where.
We are in love's hand to - day—

Our seamen are fledged Loves,
Our masts are bills of doves,
Our decks fine gold;
Our ropes are dead maids' hair,

海之恋

今天我们来到爱的大地，
将去往何方？
亲爱的，我们是开始还是停息
是扬帆远航还是小湖荡舟？
八面来风，道路条条，
不是五月胜似五月；
今天我们听凭爱来掌控；
我们将去往何方？

大地的风是哀伤的呼吸
带着亲吻死者的气息
以及那往日的欢乐；
玫瑰是航船的压舱石；
天晓得路在何方，
爱知道路在何方。
今天我们听凭爱的掌控——

水手是插上羽翼的爱神，
桅杆是鸽子的尖喙，
黄金铺满船甲，
死去少女的发丝编成缆绳，

Our stores are love - shafts fair
And manifold.
We are in love's land to - day—

Where shall we land you, sweet ?
On fields of strange men's feet,
Or fields near home?
Or where the fire - flowers blow,
Or where the flowers of snow
Or flowers of foam?
We are in love's hand to - day—

Land me, she says, where love
Shows but one shaft, one dove,
One heart, one hand.
—A shore like that, my dear,
Lies where no man will steer,
No maiden land.

爱神的箭是我们的储备；
物品齐全，应有尽有。
今天我们来到了爱的大地——

在哪里让你登岸，亲爱的？
在陌生人脚下的土地，
还是在毗邻故乡的土地？
是在火花绽放，
雪花飘舞，
浪花翻滚的地方？
今天我们听凭爱的掌控——

让我上岸，她说，在那有爱的地方，
只要有一支箭，一只鸽子
一颗心，一只手。
——像那样的海岸，亲爱的，
没有男人会驶往，
没有少女会登岸。

A Ballad of Dreamland

I hid my heart in a nest of roses,
Out of the sun's way, hidden apart;
In a softer bed than the soft white snow's is,
Under the roses I hid my heart.
Why would it sleep not? why should it start,
When never a leaf of the rose – tree stirred?
What made sleep flutter his wings and part?
Only the song of a secret bird.

Lie still, I said, for the wind's wing closes,
And mild leaves muffle the keen sun's dart;
Lie still, for the wind on the warm seas dozes,
And the wind is unquieter yet than thou art.
Does a thought in thee still as a thorn's wound smart?
Does the fang still fret thee of hope deferred?
What bids the lips of thy sleep dispart?
Only the song of a secret bird.

The green land's name that a charm encloses,
It never was writ in the traveller's chart,
And sweet on its trees as the fruit that grows is,

梦乡歌谣

把我的心掩藏在玫瑰温床里，
避开阳光，分散隐藏；
玫瑰下面，藏着我的一颗心。
藏在比白雪还软和的床榻里，
为何心儿无眠？为何心儿惊跳，
当玫瑰树上没有一片叶子舞动？
是什么让睡意挥动他的翅膀飞走？
只有一只神秘的鸟儿在歌唱。

安静躺下吧，我说，风儿的翅膀已合拢，
温柔的叶子裹住了炽热太阳投射的飞镖；
安静躺下吧，风儿正在温暖的海上打盹儿；
其实风儿比不上你平静。
你的思念还像荆棘刺伤那样剧烈？
迟来的希望仍像毒牙令你烦恼？
是什么让你睡眠中张开了双唇？
只有一只神秘的鸟儿在歌唱。

绿色大地的名字附上了一道咒文，
从不会写入旅行者的地图里，
仿佛树上结出甘美无比的果实，

It never was sold in the merchant's mart.

The swallows of dreams through its dim fields dart,

And sleep's are the tunes in its tree – tops heard;

No hound's note wakens the wildwood hart,

Only the song of a secret bird.

ENVOI

In the world of dreams I have chosen my part,

To sleep for a season and hear no word

Of true love's truth or of light love's art,

Only the song of a secret bird.

但从不会被拿到市场上出售。
梦中的燕子飞掠过昏暗的田野，
酣睡中的梦好似树梢上听到的曲调。
猎犬的音调不会唤醒森林里的雄鹿，
只有一只神秘的鸟儿在歌唱。

结尾
在梦的世界，我已选好了我的角色，
睡上长长的一个季节，哪怕听不到
一句真爱的诺言或轻薄挑逗的情话，
只有一只神秘的鸟儿在歌唱。

Gerard Manley Hopkins
杰拉德·曼利·霍普金斯

杰拉德·曼利·霍普金斯（Gerard Manley Hopkins，1844—1889）是维多利亚时代最杰出的诗人之一，被誉为那个时代最伟大的宗教诗人。霍普金斯的诗歌主题主要涉及宗教、自然和忧郁。然而，由于其诗歌创作风格与同时代诗人迥异，在世时他受欢迎程度并不高，直到第一次世界大战后他的诗歌才逐渐被读者和评论家广泛认可。他的诗歌语言充满新奇，使用了大量头韵、重音前移、古体字、意象跳跃等手段，特别是“跳跃韵”（sprung rhyme）的运用“为英国诗歌从传统向现代的转型奠定了基础”。

The Caged Skylark

As a dare - gale skylark scanted in a dull cage
Man's mounting spirit in his bone - house, mean house, dwells—
That bird beyond the remembering his free fells;
This in drudgery, day - labouring - out life's age.
Though aloft on turf or perch or poor low stage,
Both sing sometímes the sweetest, sweetest spells,
Yet both droop deadly sómetimes in their cells
Or wring their barriers in bursts of fear or rage.
Not that the sweet - fowl, song - fowl, needs no rest—
Why, hear him, hear him babble and drop down to his nest,
But his own nest, wild nest, no prison.
Man's spirit will be flesh - bound when found at best,
But uncumberèd: meadow - down is not distressed
For a rainbow footing it nor he for his bónes rísen.

笼中云雀

犹如一只勇敢在大风中翱翔的云雀囚于黑暗的鸟笼，
人类崇高的灵魂栖居在躯体简陋的寓所里——
那只鸟儿忘记了他曾自由飞翔过的山岗；
灵魂身陷奴役，必每日劳碌辛苦终生。
虽说鸟儿歇息在草皮上或栖枝上，人或身处贫穷底层，
虽然他们都会时而唱出最甜美的歌儿，
但两者却时常会在牢房里垂头丧气，
或一时暴怒或惊惧，扭断藩篱的束缚。
并非甜蜜的鸟儿，会唱歌的鸟儿就不需要窠巢——
嗨，听听他欢快的歌唱，唱完还会降落巢穴。
但那是他自己的窝，野生的巢穴，绝非牢笼。
人类灵魂复活还要寄寓肉身，
然而却少了羁绊，就如草地上蒲公英的毛绒不会烦恼，
彩虹能承载起草地毛绒，但他却承载不起人类。

Pied Beauty

Glory be to God for dappled things—
For skies of couple - color as a brinded cow;
For rose - moles all in stipple upon trout that swim;
Fresh - firecoal chestnut - falls; finches' wings;
Landscape plotted and pieced—fold, fallow, and plough;
And áll trádes, their gear and tackle and trim.
All things counter, original, spare, strange;
Whatever is fickle, freckled (who knows how?)
With swift, slow; sweet, sour; adazzle, dim;
He fathers - forth whose beauty is past change:
Praise him.

杂色之美

大千世界斑斓绚丽，当属上帝的荣耀——
双色调的天空如奶牛身上斑驳的花斑；
游动的鳟鱼点刻着玫瑰色和黑褐色斑纹；
掉落的栗子透出刚烧红的煤褐色；雀鸟的翅膀斑驳陆离；
大地的景象被分割成小块——围栏、闲耕地、可耕地；
齿轮、索具和修整机，各种营生的物件一应俱全。
万物相克而生，有的新颖、有的粗陋，还有的奇特；
各种斑点变化多端（谁知由何而来?）
快、慢、甜、酸、炫、暗，各种色调无奇不有；
杂色之美出自上帝之手，亘古不变：
赞美他吧！

Alice Meynell
爱丽丝· 梅内尔

爱丽丝·克里斯蒂娜·格特鲁德·梅内尔（Alice Christiana Gertrude Meynell，1847—1922）是英国著名随笔作家和女诗人。她出生于伦敦，在意大利度过了她的童年，后来成了一名罗马天主教徒。梅内尔受丁尼生和罗斯金影响较大，1875 年出版了第一部诗集《序曲》（*Preludes*）。梅内尔的诗歌语言简朴，表现了较为浓厚的宗教情结，常常透露出淡淡的哀伤和怀旧情愫。

Renouncement

I must not think of thee; and, tired yet strong,
I shun the love that lurks in all delight—
The love of thee—and in the blue heaven's height,
And in the dearest passage of a song.
Oh, just beyond the sweetest thoughts that throng
This breast, the thought of thee waits hidden yet bright;
But it must never, never come in sight;
I must stop short of thee the whole day long.
But when sleep comes to close each difficult day,
When night gives pause to the long watch I keep,
And all my bonds I needs must loose apart,
Must doff my will as raiment laid away, —
With the first dream that comes with the first sleep
I run, I run, I am gather'd to thy heart.

绝念

不必把你想起；我身心疲惫，却依旧顽强，
我要躲避蛰伏在所有喜悦里的爱恋——
把对你的爱搁置在蓝天之巅，
放在诗歌最亲切的章节里。
啊，超过了塞满胸膛的甜蜜情思，
对你的思念等待柳暗花明的那一刻；
但这份思念切切不可示人；
我不能终日把你挂牵。
每当艰困的日子睡意袭来，
每当黑夜容我暂停窥伺你时，
我要挣脱所有的羁绊，
如褪去衣裳一样，抛弃执念，
带着初睡的第一个梦，
奔向你，聚集在你心间。

Your Own Fair Youth

Your own fair youth, you care so little for it—
Smiling toward Heaven, you would not stay the advances
Of time and change upon your hapiest fancies.
I keep your golden hour, and will restore it.
If ever, in time to come, you would explore it—

Your old self, whose thoughts went like last year's pansies,
Look unto me; no mirror keeps its glances;
In my unfailing praises now I store it.
To guard all joys of yours from Time's estranging,
I shall then be a treasury where your gay,
Happy, and pensive past unaltered is.
I shall then be a garden charmed from changing,
In which your June has never passed away.
Walk there awhile among my memories.

美好的青春

拥有美好的青春，你却不在乎——
向天微笑，但凭你的奇思妙想，
无法阻止时间和变化前行的步伐。
我要保存你金色的年华，重新拾回它。
如果真有未来，你会去追寻它——

从前的你思绪万千，如去年的色堇已离去，
仰望着我；明镜也留不住它的反光；
我要用尽溢美之词把它珍藏。
呵护你全部的快乐不受时间的疏远，
当你永恒的快乐、幸福、沉思消散无踪，
我就将成为你的宝藏。
我会做一个魅力永恒的花园，
你的六月从未在花园中消逝，
请来我记忆的花园里漫步片刻。

Regrets

As, when the seaward ebbing tide doth pour
Out by the low sand spaces,
The parting waves slip back to clasp the shore
With lingering embraces, —

So in the tide of life that carries me
From where thy true heart dwells
Waves of my thoughts and memories turn to thee
With lessening farewell;
Waving of hands; dreams, when the day forgets;
A care half lost in cares;
The saddest of my verses; dim regrets;
Thy name among my prayers.
I would the day might come, so waited for,
So patiently besought,
When I, returning, should fill up once more
Thy desolated thought;

And fill thy loneliness that lies apart
In still, persistent pain.
Shall I content thee, O thou broken heart,
As the tide comes again,
And brims the little sea – shore lakes, and sets

遗恨

大海退潮时
海水从低矮的沙滩奔流而去，
分开的海浪逆流而回抓住海岸，
拥抱岸边不愿离去，——

如生命的潮汐从你心脏居住的地方
把我带走。
思绪和回忆的浪花涌向你，
依稀作别；
挥手告别；当白天不再梦想；
一半牵挂，一半忧愁；
我最忧伤的诗；充满淡淡的遗恨；
祈祷中呼唤你的名字。
我愿这一天来临，我等待着这一天，
耐心地乞求它到来，
当我归来，我将再一次
占据你痛苦的思念；

抚平你离别的寂寞
尽管寂寞仍隐隐作痛。
哦，你那破碎的心，还能让你称心如意？
就像海潮再次来临，
重新溢满海岸边的小湖，

Seaweeds afloat, and fills
The silent pools, rivers and rivulets
Among the inland hills?

让海草漂浮在大海上，
海水会灌满寂静的水洼、河流和小溪，
直到涌向陆地的山丘之间？

The Shepherdess

She walks—the lady of my delight—
A shepherdess of sheep.
Her flocks are thoughts. She keeps them white;
She keeps them from the steep;
She feeds them on the fragrant height,
And folds them in for sleep.

She roams maternal hills and bright,
Dark valleys safe and deep.
Into that tender breast at night
The chastest stars may peep.
She walks—the lady of my delight—
A shepherdess of sheep.

She holds her little thoughts in sight,
Though gay they run and leap.
She is so circumspect and right;
She has her soul to keep.
She walks—the lady of my delight—
A shepherdess of sheep.

牧羊女

她走过来——我可爱的姑娘，
赶着羊群的牧羊女。
羊群是念想，她养的羊儿一片洁白；
她不让羊儿去峭壁；
她在花香四溢的高地上把羊放，
让羊儿圈在栏中安睡。

她漫游在阳光明媚的山岗，
幽谷深深，平安祥和。
夜晚纯洁的星星闪现，
窥视着她软柔的胸膛。
她走过来——我可爱的姑娘，
赶着羊群的牧羊女。

她看护着她的小念想，
尽管羊儿愉快地四处跑跳。
她是那样周到细微又敏捷；
满怀热情守护着羊群。
她走过来——我可爱的姑娘，
赶着羊群的牧羊女。

Rudyard Kipling
鲁德亚德·吉卜林

约瑟夫·鲁德亚德·吉卜林（Joseph Rudyard Kipling，1865—1936）出生于印度孟买，长期生活在印度，是最杰出的英—印文学的代表人物，大英帝国忠实的吹鼓手。他的主要文学作品多在19世纪最后十年出版，1907年获得诺贝尔文学奖。除小说创作，吉卜林一生写了大量的诗歌，如《分类的歌曲》（*Departmental Ditties and Other Verses*，1886）、《七海》（*Seven Seas*，1896）等诗集。他的诗歌大都以殖民地为背景，具有浓郁的异国情调，有很多诗歌以普通士兵的生活为题材，描写他们的思想与情感。

If—

If you can keep your head when all about you
Are losing theirs and blaming it on you,
If you can trust yourself when all men doubt you,
But make allowance for their doubting too;
If you can wait and not be tired by waiting,
Or being lied about, don't deal in lies,
Or being hated, don't give way to hating,
And yet don't look too good, nor talk too wise:

If you can dream—and not make dreams your master;
If you can think—and not make thoughts your aim;
If you can meet with Triumph and Disaster
And treat those two impostors just the same;
If you can bear to hear the truth you've spoken
Twisted by knaves to make a trap for fools,
Or watch the things you gave your life to, broken,
And stoop and build'em up with worn - out tools:

If you can make one heap of all your winnings

如果……

如果你能保持头脑清醒，即便周围所有人
失去理智，纷纷责苛于你，
如果你能相信自己，即便所有人
怀疑你，你仍能顾及他们的疑虑，
如果你能等待而又不为等待感到烦躁，
或者饱受谗言，却不以谎言相向，
或者遭人忌恨，却不以恶报恶。
你既不踌躇满志，也不装腔作势：

如果你心怀梦想，却又不为梦奴役；
如果你是善思者，却又不迷失目标；
如果同时经逢胜利和失败，
而视二者同为骗徒；
如果你能忍受你的真言被歪曲，
权当那是无赖之徒为傻子设下的陷阱，
或者瞧见你毕生为之付出的事业被断送，
仍能屈尊拾起破旧的工具重新开始：

如果你能把所有胜利当作赌注，

And risk it on one turn of pitch – and – toss,
And lose, and start again at your beginnings
And never breathe a word about your loss;
If you can force your heart and nerve and sinew
To serve your turn long after they are gone,
And so hold on when there is nothing in you
Except the Will which says to them: 'Hold on!'

If you can talk with crowds and keep your virtue,
Or walk with Kings—nor lose the common touch,
If neither foes nor loving friends can hurt you,
If all men count with you, but none too much;
If you can fill the unforgiving minute
With sixty seconds' worth of distance run,
Yours is the Earth and everything that's in it,
And—which is more—you'll be a Man, my son!

在投掷游戏里孤注一掷，
如果输了，就重头再来，
但绝不轻言失败；
即便有些人早已作古，
你仍能义无反顾，恪尽职守，
尽管你已一无所有，但仍意志弥坚，
唯有意志告诉你，“坚持住。”

如果你能与庶民交谈，却持守美德，
或者与帝王同行，却不失凡人品行，
如果敌人和朋友都无法伤害你，
如果众人皆能信任你，却又不过分指望你；
如果你能以六十秒跑步的速度，
充实无情的每一分钟，
那么，大地和万物皆为你所拥有，
更重要的是，我的儿子，你将成为男子汉了！

In Springtime

My garden blazes brightly with the rose – bush and the peach,
And the koil sings above it, in the siris by the well,
From the creeper – covered trellis comes the squirrel's chattering speech,
And the blue jay screams and flutters where the cheery sat – bhai dwell.
But the rose has lost its fragrance, and the koil's note is strange;
I am sick of endless sunshine, sick of blossom – burdened bough.
Give me back the leafless woodlands where the winds of Springtime range —
Give me back one day in England, for it's Spring in England now!

Through the pines the gusts are booming, o'er the brown fields blowing chill,
From the furrow of the ploughshare streams the fragrance of the loam,
And the hawk nests on the cliffside and the jackdaw in the hill,
And my heart is back in England 'mid the sights and sounds of Home.
But the garland of the sacrifice this wealth of rose and peach is,
Ah! koil, little koil, singing on the siris bough,
In my ears the knell of exile your ceaseless bell like speech is—
Can you tell me aught of England or of Spring in England now?

在春天里

蔷薇花绽放，桃花盛开，我的花园色彩绚丽缤纷，
井边那棵合欢树上，风铃鸟不停鸣唱，
蔓枝爬满的藤架传来松鼠呜呜的叫声，
蓝色的松鸦扑打翅膀发出尖叫，欢快的八哥栖息在它的巢里。
但玫瑰不再芬芳，风铃鸟的调子那么奇特；
我已厌倦没完没了的阳光，厌弃花繁枝茂。
带我回到那没有枝叶的林地，让春风狂吹——
给我一天回到英格兰，那里正值春天！

阵阵狂风从松林咆哮而过，寒风凛冽扫过褐色的田野，
肥沃的土地散发出芳香，从犁头翻出的地沟弥漫开来，
鹰在悬崖峭壁筑巢而居，寒鸦在山岗悲鸣，
此景此声，令我心儿回到了英格兰。
玫瑰和桃子是我们的财富，是我们奉祀的花环，
啊！风铃鸟，小小的风铃鸟在合欢树上尽情地吟唱，
你经久不停的钟声似在诉说，我的耳边仿佛回响起放逐的丧钟——
能否捎来英格兰的音信或者诉说那里的春天？

Robert Louis Stevenson
罗伯特·路易斯·史蒂文森

罗伯特·路易斯·史蒂文森（Robert Louis Stevenson，1850—1894）出生在苏格兰的爱丁堡，是维多利亚时期最杰出的冒险小说作家之一。他创作的《金银岛》（*Treasure Island*，1883）、《化身博士》（*The Strange Case of Dr. Jekyll and Mr. Hyde*，1886）、《绑架》（*Kidnapped*，1886）等小说在当时风靡一时，像《金银岛》这样的作品至今仍广为流传。史蒂文森的诗歌创作主要集中在他的《一个孩子的诗园》（*A Child's Garden of Verses*，1885），他的诗歌富有幻想，充满天真浪漫的气息。

To What Shall I Compare Her

To what shall I compare her,
That is as fair as she?
For she is fairer—fairer
Than the sea.
What shall be likened to her,
The sainted of my youth?
For she is truer—truer
Than the truth.

As the stars are from the sleeper,
Her heart is hid from me;
For she is deeper – deeper
Than the sea.
Yet in my dreams I view her
Flush rosy with new ruth—
Dreams! Ah, may these prove truer
Than the truth.

我欲把她比作什么?

我欲把她比作什么，
才配得上她的美丽?
因为她更漂亮——
比大海更美丽。
我欲把她比作什么，
才配得上我圣洁的芳华?
因为她更真实
比现实更真切。

正如酣睡中的人看不见繁星点点，
她对我关闭了那扇心扉;
因为她更深沉——
比大海更深邃。
然而，唯有在梦里我才能一睹她的芳容，
新添的悲悯使她容颜红光焕发——
那毕竟是梦啊！哦，多么希望我的梦想成真，
变为现实。

Love, What Is Love

Love—what is love? A great and aching heart;
Wrung hands; and silence; and a long despair.
Life—what is life? Upon a moorland bare
To see love coming and see love depart.

何为爱情

爱情——何为爱情？是一颗美好而疼痛的心；
是曾经的牵手，今天的无语；是长久的绝望。
生活——何为生活？是身处萧条广袤的荒原
亲眼目睹爱恨别离。

Swallows Travel To and Fro

Swallows travel to and fro,
And the great winds come and go,
And the steady breezes blow,
Bearing perfume, bearing love.
Breezes hasten, swallows fly,
Towered clouds forever ply,
And at noonday, you and I
See the same sunshine above.

Dew and rain fall everywhere,
Harvests ripen, flowers are fair,
And the whole round earth is bare
To the moonshine and the sun;
And the live air, fanned with wings,
Bright with breeze and sunshine, brings
Into contact distant things,
And makes all the countries one.

Let us wander where we will,
Something kindred greets us still;
Something seen on vale or hill
Falls familiar on the heart;
So, at scent or sound or sight,

燕子飞去又飞回

燕子飞去又飞回
大风吹来又吹回，
和风徐徐吹来，
带来花香，带来爱情。
轻风催人，燕子高飞，
高天流云往返不息，
正午时分，你和我
望见头顶同一片晴空。

露水和雨水溅落四方，
年丰时稔，正值姹紫嫣红时，
浑圆的地球袒露无遗，
任凭日月光辉普照；
群鸟振翅，天空生机勃勃，
风吹阳光照，万物竟欢颜，
此地连彼地，近邻交远亲，
天下大同一家亲。

让我们自由自在云游天下，
同宗同类迎远客，
山川河谷景象万千
似曾相识印心间；
闻味，听声或睹物，

Severed souls by day and night
Tremble with the same delight—
Tremble, half the world apart.

两颗被白昼和黑夜分开的心
一样的喜悦，同样的情不自禁——
同样的情不自禁，那一半相隔遥远的世界！

Francis Thompson
弗朗西斯·汤普森

弗朗西斯·汤普森（Francis Thompson，1859—1907）是19世纪下半叶的一位诗人。他早年生活艰困，历经坎坷，直到1888年才开始诗歌写作，因此他传世的作品数量极少。汤普森的诗歌宗教意味浓厚，语言铿锵有力，意象新奇。尽管他被认为是19世纪较为重要的一位诗人，但不少批评家认为他的诗歌缺乏新意，语言冗长。诗集《天堂猎犬》（*The Hound of Heaven*，1893）被认为是他最优秀的作品。

To a Snowflake

What heart could have thought you? —
Past our devisal
(O filigree petal!)
Fashioned so purely,
Fragilely, surely,
From what Paradisal
Imagineless metal,
Too costly for cost?
Who hammered you, wrought you,
From argentine vapor? —
"God was my shaper.
Passing surmisal,
He hammered, He wrought me,
From curled silver vapor,
To lust of His mind—
Thou could'st not have thought me!
So purely, so palely,
Tinily, surely,
Mightily, frailly,
Insculped and embossed,
With His hammer of wind,
And His graver of frost."

致雪花

怎样的心思才能构思出你？
超过了我们的设想。
（哦，多么精致的花蕾！）
浑然天成，如此纯洁，
脆弱而自若，
来自天堂，
超乎想象的金属，
价值不菲？
是谁从银色气雾里，
用刀斧神功把你造就？
“是上帝塑造了我的身形。
真是难以猜到，
他用锤子敲，他把我拧成形。
用卷曲的银色水雾，
用他的激情——
你真的难以想象我！
如此纯洁，如此雪白，
如此玲珑，如此安然，
如此遒劲，如此脆弱，
真乃精雕细琢，
寒风是他的锤子，
严霜是他的刻刀。”

Dream Tryst

The breaths of kissing night and day
Were mingled in the eastern Heaven,
Throbbing with unheard melody,
Shook Lyra all its star – cloud seven.
When dusk shrank cold, and light trod shy,
And dawn's grey eyes were troubled grey;
And souls went palely up to the sky,
And mine to Lucidè,
There was no change in her sweet eyes
Since last I saw those sweet eyes shine;
There was no change in her deep heart
Since last that deep heart knocked at mine.
Her eyes were clear, her eyes were Hope's,
Wherein did ever come and go;
The sparkle of the fountain drops
From her sweet soul below.
The chambers in the house of dream
Are fed with so divine an air,
That Time's hoar wings grow young therein,
And they who walk there are most fair.
I joyed for me, I joyed for her,
Who with the Past meet girt about:
Where her last kiss still warms the air,
Nor can her eyes go out.

梦中幽会

亲吻黑夜和白昼的气息
在东边的天空中融为一体，
无声的旋律在跳动，
惊醒了天琴星座的七颗星。
黄昏退去带来几分寒意，亮光羞怯地离去，
黎明灰色的双眸流露出忧郁；
幽灵隐隐约约飞上了天空，
而我的心飞向了鲁西迪，
自从上一次见到她甜蜜明亮的双眼
看不出她迷人的眼里有何变化；
自从上一次她叩开了我的心扉
她的内心深处没有一丝变化。
她双眼明亮，充满希望：
她来自何方，又会去往何处？
从她美丽的心灵下方
溅落的泉水闪闪发光。
充满梦想的房屋的卧室
弥漫着一种神圣的气息，
时光灰白的羽翼重新变得年轻，
那里的人无比可爱。
我为自己高兴，也为她兴奋：
邂逅的故人嘲笑她：
她最后的亲吻温暖了空气，
她的目光再也不能离去。

To Olivia

I fear to love thee, Sweet, because
Love's the ambassador of loss;
White flake of childhood, clinging so
To my soiled raiment, thy shy snow
At tenderest touch will shrink and go.
Love me not, delightful child.
My heart, by many snares beguiled,
Has grown timorous and wild.
It would fear thee not at all,
Wert thou not so harmless – small.
Because thy arrows, not yet dire,
Are still unbarbed with destined fire,
I fear thee more than hadst thou stood
Full – panoplied in womanhood.

致奥利薇娅

亲爱的，我生怕爱上你，
因为爱是失败的使者；
童年时期洁白的雪花
还依附在我沾满污渍的衣裳上，
最温柔的触碰
也会让你羞涩的雪消融无踪。
不要爱我，可爱的孩子。
太多的诱惑让我的心迷失方向，
它已变得羞怯和荒凉。
它一点不惧怕你，
即使你能造成伤害，也无伤大雅。
因为你的箭一点不可怕，
它们还没有装上命运之火的利锋，
但我却非常害怕从前的你浓妆艳抹
风姿绰约站立在我眼前。

Ernest Dowson
欧尼斯特·道森

欧尼斯特·克里斯托弗·道森（Ernest Christopher Dowson，1867—1900）长期生活在伦敦，曾在牛津王后学院就读，但并没有完成学业。道森一生颇具悲剧色彩，1894 年，其父亲自杀，6 个月后，母亲又自杀，他本人因身患痨病、嗜酒，生活十分窘迫。道森是世纪末颓废文学的代表人物之一，他的诗歌多表现出对青春、爱情、美的悔恨，如单相思的痛苦便是他热衷表达的一个主题。他创作的诗歌数量不多，但他却写出了如“gone with the wind”和“days of wine and roses”这样的精美短语。

April Love

We have walked in Love's land a little way,
We have learnt his lesson a little while,
And shall we not part at the end of day,
With a sigh, a smile?

A little while in the shine of the sun,
We were twined together, joined lips forgot
How the shadows fall when day is done,
And when Love is not.

We have made no vows—there will none be broke,
Our love was free as the wind on the hill,
There was no word said we need wish unspoke,
We have wrought no ill.

So shall we not part at the end of day,
Who have loved and lingered a little while,
Join lips for the last time, go our way,
With a sigh, a smile.

四月恋歌

我们走过一段爱的旅程，
才体味到爱的真谛。
到头来，难道要带着叹息与微笑，
依依不舍？

沐浴在灿烂阳光下，
你我曾经形影不离，
曾在热吻中忘记黑夜降临，
而今爱却走到了尽头。

没有海誓山盟——哪来毁约之说，
我们的爱宛如山岗上的风儿自由自在，
我们默默无语，祝愿埋藏在心间，
我们一切安好。

天将尽，你我依依惜别，
你我曾经深情相爱，短暂徘徊，
带着叹息与微笑，让我们最后一次亲吻，
就此别过。

A Song of The Setting Sun

A song of the setting sun!
The sky in the west is red,
And the day is all but done;
While yonder up overhead,
All too soon,
There rises so cold the cynic moon.

A Song of a Winter day!
The wind of the north doth blow,
From a sky that's chill and gray,
On fields where no crops now grow,
Fields long shorn
Of bearded barley and golden corn.

A song of a faded flower!
'Twas plucked in the tender bud,
And fair and fresh for an hour,
In a Lady's hair it stood,
Now, ah! now,
Faded it lies in the dust and low.

夕阳之歌

夕阳西下，且听歌一曲！
西边的天空一片彤红，
一天将尽；
那边头顶上空，
转眼间，
升起一轮冷冷的钩月。

冬日来临，且听歌一曲！
北风劲吹，
天空阴沉，周天寒彻，
田野荒芜，
空旷寂寥，
麦穗与金色玉米已收镰。

花儿谢了，且听歌一曲！
花蕾娇嫩堪须摘，
女士头上插鲜花，
娇艳一时残花落，
啊！此时此刻！
花儿凋零入尘土。

Beyond

Love's aftermath! I think the time is now
That we must gather in, alone, apart
The saddest crop of all the crops that grow,
Love's aftermath.
Ah, sweet, —sweet yesterday, the tears that start
Can not put back the dial; this is, I trow,
Our harvesting! Thy kisses chill my heart,
Our lips are cold; averted eyes avow
The twilight of poor love: we can but part,
Dumbly and sadly, reaping as we sow,
Love's aftermath.

爱的余波

爱的余波费思量，
聚散依依终有时，
世间最苦爱情种，
爱的余波何其大。
昨日甜言蜜语，今日泪流满面，
时光难倒回，我相信这就是
我们的收获！你的亲吻凉透了我的心，
亲吻的嘴唇冰凉，游离的目光已宣告
可怜的爱已近黄昏：我们只得分手。
默默无语，伤心欲绝，因果报应，
爱的余波何其大。

Charles Dickens
查尔斯·狄更斯

查尔斯·狄更斯（Charles Dickens，1812—1870）是英国19世纪最伟大的小说家，也是批判现实主义最杰出的代表。除创作了大量优秀的长篇小说，狄更斯也写了不少优秀的诗歌。正如评论家指出，从当时的影响和经济利益考虑，像狄更斯、萨克雷和哈代这样的作家，选择了小说创作为主，但他们也十分钟情于诗歌创作，堪称优秀的诗人。

Lucy's Song

How beautiful at eventide
To see the twilight shadows pale,
Steal o'er the landscape, far and wide,
O'er stream and meadow, mound and dale!

How soft is Nature's calm repose
When ev'ning skies their cool dews weep:
The gentlest wind more gently blows,
As if to soothe her in her sleep!

The gay morn breaks,
Mists roll away,
All Nature awakes
To glorious day.
In my breast alone
Dark shadows remain;
The peace it has known
It can never regain.

露茜之歌

黄昏时分，景色多么美丽！
望见黄昏的影子一片暗淡，
悄然笼罩了辽阔的大地，
遮掩了溪流、草地、山岗和山谷。

大自然一片安宁与柔和，
夜空为冰凉的露水哭泣，
轻柔的风儿徐徐吹拂，
仿佛在抚慰睡眠中的她。

快乐的清晨开始了，
薄雾渐渐消散，
万物苏醒，
迎来美好的一天。
但在我孤独的内心里
黑暗的阴影依然驻留；
它知道这份安宁
从此不会重回大地。

These Things Shall Never Die

The pure, the bright, the beautiful,
That stirred our hearts in youth,
The impulses to wordless prayer,
The dreams of love and truth;
The longing after something's lost,
The spirit's yearning cry,
The striving after better hopes—
These things can never die.
The timid hand stretched forth to aid
A brother in his need,
A kindly word in grief's dark hour
That proves a friend indeed;
The plea for mercy softly breathed,
When justice threatens nigh,
The sorrow of a contrite heart—
These things shall never die.
Let nothing pass for every hand
Must find some work to do;
Lose not a chance to waken love—
Be firm, and just, and true;
So shall a light that cannot fade
Beam on thee from on high.
And angel voices say to thee—
These things shall never die.

这些美好的东西绝不会消失

纯洁、光明、美丽
激发了我们年轻的心，
感召我们默默祈祷，
爱与真理是我们的梦想；
失去的东西才会令人企盼，
渴望的灵魂发出呐喊，
为了更美好的希望去拼搏——
这些美好的东西绝不会消失。
伸出你羞怯的手
给患难中的兄弟施以援手，
生逢悲伤忧郁的日子，
一句温馨的话语，
方显患难见真情；
审判的日子似将来临，
柔声乞求怜悯，
悔悟的心难免充满悲伤——
这些美好的东西绝不会消失。
不要把一切视为施舍
人要为生计奔波；
不要错过唤醒爱的机会——
要坚毅，要公正，要忠实；
光明不会黯然消逝，
它将高高照亮你。
天使传声对你说——
这些美好的东西绝不会消失。

The Ivy Green

Oh, a dainty plant is the Ivy green,
That creepeth o'er ruins old!
Of right choice food are his meals, I ween,
In his cell so lone and cold.
The wall must be crumbled, the stone decayed,
To pleasure his dainty whim:
And the mouldering dust that years have made
Is a merry meal for him.
Creeping where no life is seen,
A rare old plant is the Ivy green.

Fast he stealeth on, though he wears no wings,
And a staunch old heart has he.
How closely he twineth, how tight he clings
To his friend the huge Oak Tree!
And slyly he traileth along the ground,
And his leaves he gently waves,
As he joyously hugs and crawleth round
The rich mould of dead men's graves.
Creeping where grim death hath been,
A rare old plant is the Ivy green.

常春藤

哦，常春藤，多么精美的花草，
攀缘在古老的废墟上！
吸食美味佳肴，我想，
他的居所阴冷而荒凉。
墙垣残破，岁月风蚀了石头，
但他却陶醉于美妙的幻想中：
岁月积淀的霉尘，
成了他快意的美食。
匍匐于生命的绝地，
常春藤——世所稀有的老藤！

虽然没有飞翼，他却坚定地悄悄攀爬，
他有一颗坚强的心。
他与大橡树为友，
紧紧缠绕，多么深情的依恋！
偷偷地在地上匍匐前行，
藤叶荡起柔和的绿波。
他兴奋地拥抱，深情地
围住逝者坟墓的墓碑，
他爬满阴森可怕的死神光顾之地，
常春藤——世所稀有的老藤！

Whole ages have fled and their works decayed,
And nations have scattered been;
But the stout old Ivy shall never fade,
From its hale and hearty green.
The brave old plant, in its lonely days,
Shall fatten upon the past:
For the stateliest building man can raise
Is the Ivy's food at last.
Creeping on where time has been,
A rare old plant is the Ivy green.

岁月沧桑侵蚀了它们的杰作，
多少家国已分崩离析；
但是，健硕的老藤不会枯萎，
它依然精神矍铄，生机盎然。
无畏的老藤独立不迁，
历经岁月势将根深叶茂：
人类可以筑起辉宏的大厦，
但终将变成常春藤的佳肴，
它将继续攀缘，直到时间的尽头，
常春藤——世所稀有的老藤！

Emily Jane Brontë
艾米丽·简·勃朗特

艾米丽·简·勃朗特（Emily Jane Brontë，1818—1848）是著名女作家夏洛蒂·勃朗特（Charlotte Brontë，1816—1855）的妹妹。《呼啸山庄》（*Wuthering Heights*，1847）是艾米丽创作的唯一一部小说，但作为一名诗人，艾米丽是勃朗特三姐妹中最出色的一个。人们今天能记起艾米丽主要归功于她创作的《呼啸山庄》。由于神秘主义色彩浓厚，再加上题材范围较狭窄，她的诗歌反而影响有限，提及不多。艾米丽的诗歌意象新奇，情感表达细腻，充满睿智，不愧为英语诗歌中的佼佼者。

‘Fall, Leaves, Fall’

Fall, leaves, fall; die, flowers, away;
Lengthen night and shorten day;
Every leaf speaks bliss to me
Fluttering from the autumn tree.

I shall smile when wreaths of snow
Blossom where the rose should grow;
I shall sing when night’s decay
Ushers in a drearier day.

秋叶飘落

秋叶飘落，落英缤纷；
长夜难挨，白昼苦短；
秋叶零落纷纷
片片叶儿载欢欣。

笑迎雪花漫天舞
胜似春来玫瑰开；
长夜退去当吟歌，
沉闷日子又自来。

Love and Friendship

Love is like the wild rose - briar,
Friendship like the holly - tree—
The holly is dark when the rose - briar blooms
But which will bloom most constantly?
The wild - rose briar is sweet in the spring,
Its summer blossoms scent the air;
Yet wait till winter comes again
And who will call the wild - briar fair?
Then scorn the silly rose - wreath now
And deck thee with the holly's sheen,
That when December blights thy brow
He may still leave thy garland green.

爱情与友谊

爱情好比野蔷薇，
友谊犹如冬青树，
蔷薇花开，冬青沉闷，
但孰能花开不败？
春来蔷薇花香浓，
夏来蔷薇香四溢；
若待寒冬来临时
谁还称道蔷薇美？
蔷薇花环成笑柄。
华丽冬青装扮你，
严冬摧残你花容，
但留冬青绿葱葱。

How Clear She Shines

How clear she shines! How quietly
I lie beneath her guardian light;
While heaven and earth are whispering me,
"Tomorrow, wake, but, dream to-night."
Yes, Fancy, come, my Fairy love!
These throbbing temples softly kiss;
And bend my lonely couch above
And bring me rest, and bring me bliss.

The world is going; dark world, adieu!
Grim world, conceal thee till the day;
The heart, thou canst not all subdue,
Must still resist, if thou delay!

Thy love I will not, will not share;
Thy hatred only wakes a smile;
Thy griefs may wound – thy wrongs may tear,
But, oh, thy lies shall ne'er beguile!
While gazing on the stars that glow
Above me, in that stormless sea,
I long to hope that all the woe
Creation knows, is held in thee!

她如此光彩照人

她多么光彩照人！我又如此安详
躺卧在她呵护的光亮下；
天堂和大地对我悄悄说，
“明天，要醒来，但今夜做一个梦。”
是哦，可爱的小精灵快来吧！
太阳穴咚咚跳，轻轻在吻我；
孤独地弯曲在沙发上
带给我宁静，带给我喜悦。

世界正离去；再见吧！黑暗的世界，
阴森的世界把你笼罩，直到天明；
你无法压抑你的内心，
如果你延耽，它必定要抗拒！

我不会，绝对不会分享你的爱；
你的仇恨只能唤醒微笑；
你的悲伤会伤害——你的过错会撕裂，
然而，你的谎言绝不会令我迷失！
凝视头上闪烁的星辰
大海风平浪静，
造物主知道，我深切期盼
所有的悲伤都揽入你的怀中！

And, this shall be my dream to-night;
I'll think the heaven of glorious spheres
Is rolling on its course of light
In endless bliss, through endless years;
I'll think, there's not one world above,
Far as these straining eyes can see,
Where Wisdom ever laughed at Love,
Or Virtue crouched to Infamy;

Where, writhing 'neath the strokes of Fate,
The mangled wretch was forced to smile;
To match his patience 'gainst her hate,
His heart rebellious all the while.
Where Pleasure still will lead to wrong,
And helpless Reason warn in vain;
And Truth is weak, and Treachery strong;
And Joy the surest path to Pain;
And Peace, the lethargy of Grief;
And Hope, a phantom of the soul;
And Life, a labour, void and brief;
And Death, the despot of the whole!

这便会是我今夜的梦想；
我会想，壮丽的天穹下
天堂沿着光的航线滚滚向前，
带着无限的幸福，穿过无穷岁月；
我会想，苍穹之上并无世界存在，
极目所至，
曾经看见智慧在嘲笑爱情，
或美德甘愿屈膝于声名狼藉；

在命运的击打下拼命挣扎，
伤痕累累的可怜虫在那儿强装微笑；
还试图拿他的耐心与仇恨抗争，
他那颗叛逆的心始终如一。
只要快乐还会滋生罪孽，
无助的理智就只是徒有虚名的警告；
真理会变得弱小，阴谋反会强大；
快乐不过是通往痛苦的必由之路；
安宁不过是悲伤的嗜睡虫；
希望不过是心灵的幻影；
人生短暂，辛劳且又空虚；
唯有死神才是凌驾一切的君王！

Charles Kingsley
查尔斯·金斯利

查尔斯·金斯利（Charles Kingsley，1819—1875）是英国小说家和诗人。他毕业于剑桥大学，曾担任过维多利亚女王的牧师和威尔士亲王的导师，1860—1869 年任剑桥大学近代史教授。金斯利的代表作有小说《希帕蒂亚，新敌人与一个旧面孔》（*Hypatia*，*or New Foes with an Old Face*，1853）、《向西去》（*Westward Ho*，1855）等。除小说他还创作了《水孩子》（*The Water - Babies*，*A Fairy Tale for a Land Baby*，1863）等一些儿童读物和短小精干又脍炙人口的诗歌。

Young and Old

When all the world is young, lad,
And all the trees are green;
And every goose a swan, lad,
And every lass a queen;
Then hey for boot and horse, lad,
And round the world away!
Young blood must have its course, lad,
And every dog his day.

When all the world is old, lad,
And all the trees are brown;
And all the sport is stale, lad,
And all the wheels run down;
Creep home, and take your place there,
The spent and maimed among;
God grant you find one face there,
You loved when all was young.

年轻与年长

小伙儿，当世界还年轻，
万木苍翠；
每一只鹅都成了一只天鹅，小伙儿，
每一位少女都成了一个女王；
嘿，小伙儿，穿上靴子，骑上马，
去周游世界吧！
小伙儿，年轻人一定要走自己的路，
凡人都有出头的那一天。

小伙儿，当世界变老时，
万木枯黄；
一切欢悦不再新鲜，小伙儿，
所有的车轮破烂不堪；
那时，只好缓步回家颐养天年，
你已筋疲力尽，伤痕累累；
上帝赐予你找到一张面孔，
当一切还年轻，你的心充满爱。

The Three Fishers

Three fishers went sailing away to the west,
Away to the west as the sun went down;
Each thought on the woman who loved him the best,
And the children stood watching them out of the town;
For men must work, and women must weep,
And there's little to earn, and many to keep,
Though the harbour bar be moaning.

Three wives sat up in the lighthouse tower,
And they trimmed the lamps as the sun went down;
They looked at the squall, and they looked at the shower,
And the night-rack came rolling up ragged and brown.
But men must work, and women must weep,
Though storms be sudden, and waters deep,
And the harbour bar be moaning.

Three corpses lay out on the shining sands
In the morning gleam as the tide went down,
And the women are weeping and wringing their hands
For those who will never come home to the town;
For men must work, and women must weep,
And the sooner it's over, the sooner to sleep;
And good-bye to the bar and its moaning.

三个渔夫

三个渔夫驾船向西而去，
去向那太阳西沉的西方；
深爱他的女人记挂心间，
孩子们驻足目送他们出城远去；
男人天生不辞劳顿，女人天生哭哭啼啼，
收入微薄难以为继，
哪怕海港的沙洲在呻吟。

三个妻子端坐在灯塔里，
夕阳西下，她们点亮塔灯；
放眼大海，狂风四起，暴雨倾盆，
夜行的支架被风卷起摔得七零八落。
男人天生不辞劳顿，女人天生哭哭啼啼，
哪怕暴风雨骤起，风急浪高，
海港的沙洲在呻吟。

晨光泛起，海潮退去，
三具尸体躺卧在沙滩上，
女人们潸然泪下，扼腕痛惜，
所爱的人永远不能回到小镇，回到家了；
男人天生不辞劳顿，女人天生哭哭啼啼，
哀伤烟消云散，人们很快又酣然入睡；
作别沙洲，告别呻吟。

A Hope

Twin stars, aloft in ether clear,
Around each other roll alway,
Within one common atmosphere
Of their own mutual light and day.
And myriad happy eyes are bent
Upon their changeless love alway;
As, strengthened by their one intent,
They pour the flood of life and day.
So we through this world's waning night
May, hand in hand, pursue our way;
Shed round us order, love, and light,
And shine unto the perfect day.

希望

两颗星星高悬明净的天空，
一直围绕彼此相互旋转，
在同一片天空里
相互分享光明和白昼。
无数双兴奋的眼睛在注视
他们永恒不变的爱恋；
为一个共有的心愿，他们变得强大，
把生命和白昼的洪流倾洒大地。
穿过正在消散的黑夜世界，
愿我们手牵手，追寻我们的目标；
把和谐、爱情和光明撒满四周，
照亮最完美的一天。

William Makepeace Thackeray
威廉·麦克皮斯·萨克雷

威廉·麦克皮斯·萨克雷（William Makepeace Thackeray，1811—1863）出生在印度加尔各答，五岁时其父去世，之后才回到英国就学。萨克雷是英国19世纪杰出的批判现实主义作家之一，他的代表作《名利场》（*Vanity Fair*，1847—1848）至今仍然是英语文学的经典小说之一。萨克雷还在三一学院当学生时就开始尝试诗歌创作，他时常写一些诗歌、民谣、滑稽诗和模仿诗在 *Punch* 杂志上发表。萨克雷的诗歌轻松诙谐，优美而富有节奏感。

Sorrows of Werther

Werther had a love for Charlotte
Such as words could never utter;
Would you know how first he met her?
She was cutting bread and butter.

Charlotte was a married lady,
And a moral man was Werther,
And, for all the wealth of Indies,
Would do nothing for to hurt her.

So he sighed and pined and ogled,
And his passion boiled and bubbled,
Till he blew his silly brains out,
And no more was by it troubled.

Charlotte, having seen his body
Borne before her on a shutter,
Like a well – coducted person,
Went on cutting bread and butter.

少年维特的烦恼

维特深爱夏绿蒂
知心话儿难启齿；
初次相遇孰知晓？
绿蒂忙着切面包。

绿蒂已为他人妇，
翩翩君子属维特，
家有万贯徒奈何，
怎能忍心伤害她。

暗恋情深人憔悴，
欲火焚身难自拔，
糊涂自绝寻短见，
从此不再寻烦恼。

躺卧门板气奄奄，
绿蒂何忍送君别，
品行无邪为良妇，
赓续故作切面包。

Serenade

Now the toils of day are over,
And the sun hath sunk to rest,
Seeking, like a fiery lover,
The bosom of the blushing west—

The faithful night keeps watch and ward,
Raising the moon her silver shield,
And summoning the stars to guard
The slumbers of my fair Mathilde!

The faithful night! Now all things lie
Hid by her mantle dark and dim,
In pious hope I hither hie,
And humbly chant mine ev'ning hymn.

Thou art my prayer, my saint, my shrine!
(For never holy pilgrim kneel'd,
Or wept at feet more pure than thine),
My virgin love, my sweet Mathilde!

小夜曲

一日辛劳结束，
太阳西沉安息，
像一位热情的恋人，
追寻红色西天的胸怀——

忠实的夜守护着，
月亮托起银色的盾牌，
召唤群星来守护
我可爱的玛蒂尔德安然入眠！

忠实的夜！
她黑色阴暗的披风淹没了一切，
我怀着虔诚的希望四处奔走，
谦卑地为我的玛蒂尔德唱响夜的赞美诗。

你是我的祈祷者，我的圣人，我的圣坛！
（因为虔诚的朝拜者从不下跪，
或比你更纯洁地伫立而泣），
我纯洁的爱人，我可爱的玛蒂尔德！

Come to the Greenwood Tree

Come to the greenwood tree,
Come where the dark woods be,
Dearest, O come with me!
Let us rove—O my love—O my love!

Come—'tis the moonlight hour,
Dew is on leaf and flower,
Come to the linden bower, —
Let us rove—O my love—O my love!

Dark is the wood, and wide
Dangers, they say, betide;
But, at my Albert's side,
Nought I fear, O my love—O my love!

Welcome the greenwood tree,
Welcome the forest free,
Dearest, with thee, with thee,
Nought I fear, O my love—O my love!

快快来到绿林中

快快来到绿林中，
这儿绿树成荫，
亲爱的，哦，与我一道来！
让我们去流浪，哦，我的爱——哦，我的爱！

来吧——月光照亮的时候，
露珠挂满花叶，
快来菩提树荫下，
让我们去流浪，哦，我的爱——哦，我的爱！

无边树林黑茫茫，
他们说，危险将降临；
但是有我的阿尔贝特在身旁，
我无所畏惧，哦，我的爱——哦，我的爱！

欢迎来到绿林中，
欢迎来到森林里，
最亲爱的，与你一起，与你一起，
我无所畏惧，哦，我的爱——哦，我的爱！

George Eliot
乔治·爱略特

乔治·爱略特（George Eliot，1819—1880）是玛丽·安·伊凡丝（Mary Ann Evans）的笔名，英国19世纪最杰出的女小说家之一。《米德尔马契》（*Middlemarch*，1872）是她创作的最优秀的小说。与同时代许多作家一样，爱略特一直渴望在其他文学类型的创作中有所建树，她出版的两部诗集在她那个时代为她赢得了不少赞誉，但她的诗歌并未引起现当代批评家应有的关注。爱略特的诗歌创作承袭了她小说中的一些因素，很多诗歌的主题可以在她的小说中找到源头。

Count That Day Lost

If you sit down at set of sun
And count the acts that you have done,
And, counting, find
One self-denying deed, one word
That eased the heart of him who heard,
One glance most kind
That fell like sunshine where it went—
Then you may count that day well spent.

But if, through all the livelong day,
You've cheered no heart, by yea or nay—
If, through it all
You've nothing done that you can trace
That brought the sunshine to one face—
No act most small
That helped some soul and nothing cost—
Then count that day as worse than lost.

盘点过去的一天

如果你坐看落日
细数你的所作所为，
盘点细数，便会发现
一个无私的行为，
一句让他听后舒畅无比的话语，
亲切的一瞥
让人感觉如阳光普照——
你会认为那一天算是不负年华。

但如果你度过一整天
无论怎样做都无法激励人心，
如果度过一天
你回头追溯所做的一切
没有带来一张笑脸，
没有一桩善行，哪怕是小小的一桩，
不花一文钱，去拯救一个灵魂，
那一天算是蹉跎时光。

In a London Drawingroom

The sky is cloudy, yellowed by the smoke.
For view there are the houses opposite
Cutting the sky with one long line of wall
Like solid fog: far as the eye can stretch
Monotony of surface & of form
Without a break to hang a guess upon.
No bird can make a shadow as it flies,
For all is shadow, as in ways o'erhung
By thickest canvass, where the golden rays
Are clothed in hemp. No figure lingering
Pauses to feed the hunger of the eye
Or rest a little on the lap of life.
All hurry on & look upon the ground,
Or glance unmarking at the passers by
The wheels are hurrying too, cabs, carriages
All closed, in multiplied identity.
The world seems one huge prison – house & court
Where men are punished at the slightest cost,
With lowest rate of colour, warmth & joy.

在伦敦的一间客厅

乌云密布，烟雾染黄了天空。
看一眼对面的房屋
似一长排围墙划破天空，
也仿佛是凝固的烟雾：目光所及
全是单调的外形和结构
没有一点变调能勾起幻想。
鸟儿飞过留不下任何影子，
所有一切都成了阴影，就像是
厚厚的画布悬挂天际，
金色光线也被大麻包裹，没有行人
踯躅停步去一饱眼福，
或者停留在生活的环抱中。
路人行色匆匆，埋头盯着地面。
或漫不经心偷看路上的过客。
车轮在疾驶，出租车、马车
都关着窗户，如出一辙。
整个世界似一座巨大的牢房和法庭
芸芸众生在那里统统被从轻发落，
世界缺少了杂色，缺少了热情和欢乐。

Spring Comes Hither

Spring comes hither
Buds the rose...
Roses wither
Sweet spring goes ...
O ja là
O ja là ...
Would she carry me.

Summer soars
Wide – wing'd day ...
White light pours
Flies away ...
O ja là
O ja là ...
Would he carry me.

Soft winds blow
Westward borne ...
Onward go
Towards the morn
O ja là
O ja là ...
Would they carry me.

春天到这里

春天来到这里
玫瑰吐出新蕾……
玫瑰花儿凋谢
美好的春天难留……
但愿
但愿……
愿她带上我。

夏日飞升来到
伸开它那宽大的羽翼……
皓白光焰倾泻
盛夏飞逝不再
但愿
但愿……
愿他带上我。

轻风徐徐吹过
载我一路西行……
一步一步向前
迎接东方黎明
但愿
但愿……
愿他们带上我。

Sweet birds sing
O'er the graves
Then take wing
O'er the waves
O ja là
O ja là...
Would they carry me.

甜蜜鸟儿吟唱
坟头悲鸣不止
鸟儿振翅飞翔
掠过滔滔白浪
但愿
但愿……
愿他们带上我。

Edward Fitzgerald
爱德华· 菲兹杰拉德

爱德华 · 菲兹杰拉德（Edward Fitzgerald, 1809—1883）英国诗人、翻译家。作为一个诗人，经他一手创作的诗屈指可数，其地位主要归功于他翻译的《鲁拜集》（*Rubáiyát of Omar Khayyám*, 1859）。这部作品远远超过了单纯的字面翻译，而更像一种释义、一种创造性的翻译。这部诗集因深切迎合了维多利亚人世纪末的悲观情绪曾经风靡一时。菲兹杰拉德的著作还包括《幼发拉底人》（*Euphranor*, 1851）和《波洛尼厄斯》（*Polonius*, 1852），前者采用苏格拉底式的对话来评论教育体系，后者是一本格言集。

Old Song

TIS a dull sight
To see the year dying,
When winter winds
Set the yellow wood sighing:
Sighing, O sighing!

When such a time cometh
I do retire
Into an old room
Beside a bright fire:
O, pile a bright fire!

And there I sit
Reading old things,
Of knights and lorn damsels,
While the wind sings—
O, drearily sings!

I never look out
Nor attend to the blast;
For all to be seen
Is the leaves falling fast:
Falling, falling!

一首老歌

沉闷的光景
眼瞅着一年又到尽头，
冬天的寒风刮过，
萎黄的树木发出悲鸣：
呜呜，哦，呜呜！

这样的日子来临，
我只得退避而居
回到那间老屋，
围坐在明亮的炉火旁：
哦，燃起旺旺的火堆！

在那儿独自坐定，
读一些旧闻逸事，
骑士和孤单的少女的故事，
风儿轻轻吟唱——
哦，多么单调的歌儿！

从不看窗外，
也不必在意疾风吹；
但见得
落叶纷纷飘落：
叶儿落，叶儿落！

But close at the hearth,
Like a cricket, sit I,
Reading of summer
And chivalry—
Gallant chivalry!

Then with an old friend
I talk of our youth—
How 't was gladsome, but often
Foolish, forsooth:
But gladsome, gladsome!

Or, to get merry,
We sing some old rhyme
That made the wood ring again
In summer time—
Sweet summer time!

Then go we smoking,
Silent and snug:
Naught passes between us,
Save a brown jug—
Sometimes!

And sometimes a tear
Will rise in each eye,
Seeing the two old friends
So merrily—
So merrily!

And ere to bed

紧挨着炉膛，
像一只蟋蟀就座，
读夏日炎炎，
读骑士风采——
多么勇敢的骑士！

与老友攀谈，
谈起我们的青春——
年轻时多么令人兴奋，
又实实在在是愚蠢：
但谈起就兴奋，兴奋！

或为助兴，
我们唱起老词儿，
歌声又在林间回响，
夏日时光——
多么美妙的夏日时光！

有时我们抽起烟来，
默默无语但心中惬意：
我们之间没有什么传来递去，
除了传杯弄盏——
时而也要把酒言欢！

时而，泪水夺目，
两眼热泪盈眶，
得见两位老友，
乐哉——
乐哉！

临睡之前，

Go we, go we,
Down on the ashes
We kneel on the knee,
Praying together!

Thus, then, live I
Till, 'mid all the gloom,
By Heaven! the bold sun
Is with me in the room
Shining, shining!

Then the clouds part,
Swallows soaring between;
The spring is alive,
And the meadows are green!
I jump up like mad,
Break the old pipe in twain,
And away to the meadows,
The meadows again!

让我们一道过去，
跪在灰烬上，
双膝跪地，
一道虔诚祈祷！

因此，我快活地活着，
直到度过那些阴暗的日子，
上天保佑！耀眼的太阳
终于与我同在一室了
阳光明媚，明媚阳光！

云散了，
燕子在云际之间翱翔；
春天生机勃勃，
草地绿了！
我癫狂地跳跃，
把烟斗折成两截，
冲向草地，
草地又回来了！

To a Violet

Fair violet! sweet saint!
Answer us—Whither art thou gone?
Ever thou wert so still, and faint,
And fearing to be look'd upon.
We cannot say that one hath died,
Who wont to live so unespied,
But crept away unto a stiller spot,
Where men may stir the grass, and find thee not.

致紫罗兰

可爱的紫罗兰！多么圣洁的花！
请你回答我们——你到哪儿去了？
你永远如此安详，如此娇小，
胆怯于被人窥探。
没有人会说它已死亡，
它习惯静静地活着，而不让人察觉，
悄悄爬到一个更僻静的地方，
即便有人翻动杂草，也难寻觅你的踪迹。

Lewis Carroll
刘易斯·卡洛尔

刘易斯·卡洛尔（Lewis Carroll, 1832—1898）是查尔斯·鲁特维奇·道奇森（Charles Lutwidge Dodgson）的笔名，是英国著名的小说家、数学家和逻辑学家。童话作品《爱丽丝漫游奇境记》（*Alice in Wonderland*, 1865）是他获得崇高声望最重要的一部作品，至今深受各国儿童喜爱，爱丽丝已经成了一个家喻户晓的人物形象。卡洛尔也创作了一些脍炙人口的诗歌，如《猎鲨记》（*The Hunting of Snark*，1876）等。他善于在诗歌中营造奇幻色彩，利用文字游戏和逻辑丰富诗歌内涵。

Life Is but a Dream

A boat, beneath a sunny sky
Lingering onward dreamily
In an evening of July—

Children three that nestle near,
Eager eye and willing ear,
Pleased a simple tale to hear—

Long has paled that sunny sky;
Echoes fade and memories die;
Autumn frosts have slain July.

Still she haunts me, phantomwise,
Alice moving under skies
Never seen by waking eyes.

Children yet, the tale to hear,
Eager eye and willing ear,
Lovingly shall nestle near.

In a Wonderland they lie,
Dreaming as the days go by,
Dreaming as the summers die;

人生不过一场梦

晴空下，一只小船
梦幻般地踯躅前行
在七月的一个夜晚——

三个小孩依偎在一块儿，
期盼的眼神，听话的耳朵，
一听到童话故事就兴奋——

朗朗的天空早已暗淡；
回声远去，记忆消退；
秋天的风霜屠杀了七月。

她仍像幻影萦绕于心，
爱丽丝还在漫游四方
醒来时眼睛却看不见。

但孩子们还要听故事，
期盼的眼神，听话的耳朵，
亲密地依靠在一起。

他们躺在仙境中，
岁月流逝梦不断，
夏天逝去梦依旧；

Ever drifting down the stream—
Lingering in the golden gleam—
Life, what is it but a dream?

顺着小溪一直漂——
徜徉在金色闪光里——
人生，不过梦一场？

You Are Old Father William

"You are old, Father William," the young man said,
"And your hair has become very white;
And yet you incessantly stand on your head—
Do you think, at your age, it is right?

"In my youth," Father William replied to his son,
"I feared it might injure the brain;
But now that I'm perfectly sure I have none,
Why, I do it again and again."

"You are old," said the youth, "as I mentioned before,
And you have grown must uncommonly fat;
Yet you turned a back-somersault in at the door—
Pray, what is the reason of that?"

"In my youth," said the sage, as he shook his gray locks,
"I kept all my limbs very supple
By the use of this ointment—one shilling a box—
Allow me to sell you a couple."

"You are old," said the youth, "and your jaws are too weak
For anything tougher than suet;
Yet you finished the goose, with the bones and the beak—

你老了，威廉，父亲

“威廉，父亲，你老了，”年轻人说，
“你已满头白发；
但你还不停做倒立——
都这把年纪了，你觉得合适？”

“我年轻时，”威廉父亲回答儿子道，
“我担心倒立会伤着头；
但现在我完全肯定，我一点没伤着，
哎呀，我还可以连续做倒立。”

“你老了，”年轻人说，“之前我提到过，
你已超乎寻常的胖了；
但你还要翻着筋斗进门来——
请问，那是为什么？”

“我年轻时，”智者摇摇长满白发的头道，
“我四肢非常灵活
用的就是这种药膏，一个先令一盒——
让我卖两盒给你。”

“你老了，”年轻人说，“你的下颌软弱无力
只配吃软和的板油；
但你居然干掉了一只鹅，连头和鹅嘴都没剩——

Pray, how did you manage to do it?"

"In my youth," said his father, "I took to the law,
And argued each case with my wife;
And the muscular strength, which it gave to my jaw,
Has lasted the rest of my life."

"You are old," said the youth, "one would hardly suppose
That your eyes was as steady as ever;
Yet you balanced an eel on the end of your nose—
What made you so awfully clever?"

"I have answered three questions, and that is enough,"
Said his father, "don't give yourself airs!
Do you think I can listen all day to such stuff?
Be off, or I'll kick you downstairs!"

请问，你如何吃得下？”

“我年轻时，”他的父亲说，“我迷恋法律，
和我妻子争辩每一件案子；
练就了肌肉，我下巴很有劲，
一直持续到我余生。”

“你老了，”年轻人说，“没有人能假设
你的眼神还如从前那样镇定自若；
但你能把一条鳗鱼竖立在你的鼻尖上——
是什么让你如此身手不凡？”

“我答完了三个问题，足够多了，”
他的父亲说，“千万别自个装神气！
你以为我愿意整天听这些胡说八道？
赶快滚蛋，要不，我一脚把你踢下楼！”

My Fairy

I have a fairy by my side
Which says I must not sleep,
When once in pain I loudly cried
It said "You must not weep"
If, full of mirth, I smile and grin,
It says "You must not laugh"
When once I wished to drink some gin
It said "You must not quaff" .

When once a meal I wished to taste
It said "You must not bite"
When to the wars I went in haste
It said "You must not fight" .

"What may I do?" at length I cried,
Tired of the painful task.
The fairy quietly replied,
And said "You must not ask" .

我的小精灵

我身边有一个小精灵，
说我不得睡觉，
每当我疼痛得大声喊叫
它就说，“不要哭泣”
如果满怀欢喜，我想要微笑，甚至露齿而笑，
它就说，“一定不要开口大笑”
每当我想要饮点杜松子酒
它就说，“不准狂饮”。

每当我想要尝尝佳肴的味道
它就说，“不得大快朵颐”
当我正要匆匆奔赴战场
它就说，“不要去打仗”。

“我可以做什么呢?”我终于吼道，
我已厌烦了这恼人的苦差，
小精灵平静又温和地应答道，
“不要问。”

Coventry Patmore
考文垂·帕特莫尔

考文垂·克西·迪顿·帕特莫尔（Coventry Kersey Dighton Patmore，1823—1896）的第一部诗集出版于1844年，他由此获得了在大英博物馆的助理图书管理员的职位。帕特莫尔早期的诗歌缺乏生气，多表达一些伤感的主题；他后期创作风格变化较大，主题变得更深刻、更大胆，语言也较华丽。他的主要代表作是四卷本的《屋子里的天使》（*The Angel in the House*，1854，1856，1860，1863）、《未知的厄洛斯》（*The Unknown Eros*，1877）以及《论英语韵律的法则》（*Essay on English Metrical Law*，1877）。

The Year

The crocus, while the days are dark,
Unfolds its saffron sheen;
At April's touch, the crudest bark
Discovers gems of green.

Then sleep the seasons, full of might;
While slowly swells the pod
And rounds the peach, and in the night
The mushroom bursts the sod.

The winter falls; the frozen rut
Is bound with silver bars;
The snowdrift heaps against the hut,
And night is pierced with stars.

年

天色晦暗时，番红花
绽放出橘黄色光芒；
粗糙的树皮一经四月轻点
尽显翠绿菁华。

四季憩睡是为蓄满力量；
豆荚渐渐鼓胀
绕满碧绿桃树，一夜之间
蘑菇冲破了草皮。

冬天降临；封冻的凹槽
挂满了银色的冰条；
小屋托起一堆堆白雪 ，
繁星刺破了夜空。

The Foreign Land

A woman is a foreign land,
Of which, though there he settle young,
A man will ne'er quite understand
The customs, politics, and tongue.

The foolish hie them post – haste through,
See fashions odd, and prospects fair,
Learn of the language, "How d'ye do,"
And go and brag they have been there.

The most for leave to trade apply,
For once, at Empire's seat, her heart,
Then get what knowledge ear and eye
Glean chancewise in the life – long mart.

And certain others, few and fit,
Attach them to the Court, and see
The Country's best, its accent hit,
And partly sound its polity.

陌生的土地

女人是一块陌生的土地，
男人虽说年轻时在那儿驻留，
但永远都不会深谙
那里的风俗、权谋和言语。

愚者心急火燎穿过这片土地，
只瞧见了奇装异服，景色迷人，
才学会说，“你好吗?”
就要离开，还夸口曾去过那儿。

生意场上的男人大多已离场而去，
因她曾一心垂涎帝国的宝座，
耳目即便获取一点见闻，
也只不过是人生交易场上碰了运气。

还有其他屈指可数的几个如意者，
靠攀附于王公贵胄，
投合了它的乡音，才目睹到了倾国之美，
窥见了它健全的机体。

A Farewell

With all my will, but much against my heart,
We two now part.
My Very Dear,
Our solace is, the sad road lies so clear.
It needs no art,
With faint, averted feet
And many a tear,
In our opposèd paths to persevere.
Go thou to East, I West.
We will not say
There 's any hope, it is so far away.
But, O, my Best,
When the one darling of our widowhead,
The nursling Grief,
Is dead,
And no dews blur our eyes
To see the peach - bloom come in evening skies,
Perchance we may,
Where now this night is day,
And even through faith of still averted feet,
Making full circle of our banishment,
Amazèd meet;

分手

我意已决，却心有不甘，
我俩就此分道扬镳。
我的至爱，
前路忧伤，聊以慰藉。
无须高超技艺，
拖着无力而弯曲的脚
满含泪水，
我们相对而行，百折不回。
你我各奔西东。
你我心照不宣
希望渺茫，道路迢迢，
不过，哦！我的最爱，
我们独守一室的时候，
我们精心培育的宝贝格瑞夫（悲伤），
死去了，
露珠无法模糊我们的双眼
黄昏的天空下分明看见桃花盛开，
这或许只是偶然，
这儿的夜晚也变成了白昼，
尽管我们仍步履蹒跚，但深怀信念，
圆满结束了我们的放逐，
才有了这意外的相逢；

The bitter journey to the bourne so sweet
Seasoning the termless feast of our content
With tears of recognition never dry.

历经苦涩之旅，终于来到甜美的小溪
心满意足饱享一顿丰盛的宴席
相识之时，泪湿衣襟。

Lionel Johnson
莱昂内尔·约翰逊

莱昂内尔·皮格特·约翰逊（Lionel Pigot Johnson，1867—1902）是19世纪后半叶的诗人、随笔作家和批评家。因身处世纪末，受当时那种颓废和忧郁的情绪影响，他曾被看作是19世纪末“悲惨的一代”的典型代表人物。《黑色天使》（*The Dark Angel*，1893）是约翰逊的代表作品。约翰逊的诗歌严谨、深沉、充满热情，大多抒发了他个人内心世界的情感体验。

The Precept of Silence

I know you: solitary griefs,
Desolate passions, aching hours!
I konw you: tremulous beliefs,
Agonzised hopes, and ashen flowers!

The winds are sometimes sad to me;
The starry spaces, full of fear;
Mine is the sorrow on the sea,
And mine the sigh of places drear.

Some players upon plaintive strings,
Publish their wistfulness abroad:
I have not spoken of these things,
Save to one man, and unto God.

沉默的戒律

我认识你：孤独的悲伤，
凄切的情愫，伤心的时刻！
我认识你：摇摆不定的信念，
令人痛苦的希望，死灰似的花儿！

风儿时而令我忧伤：
繁星闪烁的夜空，充满恐惧；
大海倾诉着我的悲伤，
阴郁的地方令我悲叹。

有人弹起哀怨的琴弦，
把他们的惆怅远播海外：
我却缄默无语，
因我只对上帝一个人倾诉。

July

Summer lightening, and rich rain:
Roses perfume the hot air.
All the breathless night is faint,
All the flowery night is fair.
Philomel her joy or plaint,
Sings, sings, and sings again.

What comes now? The earth awaits
What fierce wonder from the skies?
Thunder, trampling through the night?
Morning, with illustrious eyes?
Morning, from the springs of light:
Thunder, round Heaven's opening gates.

七月

夏日电光闪烁，雨水充沛：
潮热的空气弥漫着玫瑰花香。
窒息的夜晚令人昏昏欲睡，
鲜花开放的夜晚最美好。
夜莺在欢歌，夜莺在哀啼，
呖呖，呖呖，一遍遍吟唱。

是什么要来临？大地在静候
是什么凶猛的惊奇会从天而降？
是惊雷掠过夜空？
是清晨睁开明亮的双眼？
清晨来自光明的春天：
惊雷徘徊在天堂敞开的大门口。

To a Traveller

THE mountains, and the lonely death at last
Upon the lonely mountains: O strong friend!
The wandering over, and the labour passed,
Thou art indeed at rest:
Earth gave thee of her best,
That labour and this end.

Earth was thy mother, and her true son thou:
Earth called thee to a knowledge of her ways,
Upon the great hills, up the great streams: now
Upon earth's kindly breast
Thou art indeed at rest:
Thou, and thine arduous days.

Fare thee well, O strong heart! The tranquil night
Looks calmly on thee: and the sun pours down
His glory over thee, O heart of might!
Earth gives thee perfect rest:
Earth, whom thy swift feet pressed:
Earth, whom the vast stars crown.

致旅行者

翻过崇山峻岭，孤独的死亡终于来临
在孤独的群山上：哦，坚强的朋友！
流浪的日子结束了，艰辛的劳碌过去了，
你的确应该安歇了：
大地把她的精华赐予了你
——那些付出的辛劳和最终的归宿。

大地是你的母亲，你是她真正的儿子：
大地呼唤你去认识她的道路，
在巍峨的群山上，在宽广的河流上：
此时在大地慈爱的胸膛上
你的确该安歇了：
你，还有那苦日子终于熬到了尽头。

再见了，哦，强壮的心脏！静谧的夜晚
安详地注视你：太阳把它的荣耀
倾泻在你身上，哦，强大的心脏！
大地给了你最完美的宁静。
你矫健的脚步踩在大地上：
浩瀚的星空为大地戴上王冠。

Oscar Wilde
奥斯卡·王尔德

奥斯卡·王尔德（Oscar Wilde，1854—1900）生于爱尔兰都柏林，曾在三一学院和牛津大学攻读文学。他早年深受同时代散文家、唯美主义代表人物沃尔特·佩特（Walter Pater，1839—1894）影响，提出了“为艺术而艺术”的唯美主义主张。王尔德的文学创作涉及诗歌、小说、戏剧、散文和文学批评，是19世纪英国唯美主义及颓废文学的集大成者。王尔德的主要成就还在于他的小说创作，如《道林·格雷的画像》（*The Picture of Dorian Gray*，1891）。1881年，王尔德出版了第一部诗作《诗集》（*Poems*），他的诗歌继承了“先拉斐尔派”的一些传统，但主要还是阐释他的唯美主义思想。

The Grave Of Keats

Rid of the world's injustice, and his pain,
He rests at last beneath God's veil of blue:
Taken from life when life and love were new
The youngest of the martyrs here is lain,
Fair as Sebastian, and as early slain.
No cypress shades his grave, no funeral yew,
But gentle violets weeping with the dew
Weave on his bones an ever – blossoming chain.
O proudest heart that broke for misery!
O sweetest lips since those of Mitylene!
O poet – painter of our English Land!
Thy name was writ in water—it shall stand:
And tears like mine will keep thy memory green,
As Isabella did her Basil – tree.

济慈之墓

摆脱了世间的不公，摆脱了身心痛苦，
他终于安息在上帝蓝色的面纱下：
生命与爱情鲜活的时候，他撒手人寰。
最年轻的殉道者长眠于此，
如塞巴斯蒂安一样英俊，亦如他一样英年早逝。
没有松柏，没有紫杉为他的墓撑起一片绿荫，
却有高雅的紫罗兰滴下露珠为他哭泣，
鲜花编织的长链紧紧缠绕他的坟墓，
哦，你高傲的心早已痛苦欲碎！
哦，你有自古希腊先贤以来最甜蜜的唇！
哦，你是英国大地上杰出的诗人和画家！
尽管你的名字写在水上——但它将万古流芳：
像我一样哭泣的泪水将使你的记忆万古长青，
就如伊莎贝拉为她爱人种下的留兰香。

Her Voice

The wild bee reels from bough to bough
With his furry coat and his gauzy wing.
Now in a lily – cup, and now
Setting a jacinth bell a – swing,
In his wandering;
Sit closer love: it was here I trow
I made that vow.

Swore that two lives should be like one
As long as the sea – gull loved the sea,
As long as the sunflower sought the sun,
It shall be, I said, for eternity
'Twixt you and me!
Dear friend, those times are over and done,
Love's web is spun.

Look upward where the poplar trees
Sway and sway in the summer air,
Here in the valley never a breeze
Scatters the thistledown, but there
Great winds blow fair
From the mighty murmuring mystical seas,
And the wave – lashed leas.

她的声音

那只野蜜蜂从一根树枝到另一树枝绕来绕去，
他披着毛茸茸的皮毛，长着薄纱般的翅膀。
一会儿在百合花上飞舞，
一会儿又停留在摇摆的橘红色时钟上，
他四处游荡；
紧紧贴在爱的身上：它就在这儿，我相信，
我敢发誓。

我敢相信：两个生命将融为一体
只要海鸥爱大海，
只要葵花追逐太阳，
相爱到永远，我说，
把你和我捆缚在一起！
亲爱的朋友，那些时光一去不复返，
爱的罗网已织就。

抬头望杨树生长的地方
它们在夏日的天空里摇曳，
山谷里没有一丝风儿吹
蓟花的冠毛飞散八方，
这儿唯有大风狂吹
从咆哮的神秘大海
从海浪拍打的草地。

Look upward where the white gull screams,
What does it see that we do not see?
Is that a star? or the lamp that gleams
On some outward voyaging argosy,
Ah! can it be
We have lived our lives in a land of dreams!
How sad it seems.

Sweet, there is nothing left to say
But this, that love is never lost,
Keen winter stabs the breasts of May
Whose crimson roses burst his frost,
Ships tempest – tossed
Will find a harbour in some bay,
And so we may.

And there is nothing left to do
But to kiss once again, and part,
Nay, there is nothing we should rue,
I have my beauty, —you your Art,
Nay, do not start,
One world was not enough for two
Like me and you.

抬眼望去，白色的海鸥在尖叫，
它看见了什么，我却没看到？
那是一颗星星？或是一盏明灯
正照亮出海远航的大商船，
啊！可能正是它。
我们生活在梦的土地上！
似乎多么悲哀。

亲爱的，已无话可说了
除了这句话，永远不会失去爱，
凛冽的冬天刺穿五月的胸膛
绯红的玫瑰冲破了严霜，
船儿在暴风雨中摇晃
但终会找到避风的海港，
我们也一样能找到爱的港湾。

无事可做了
再一次吻别，
除此以外，我们应该没什么可后悔了，
我拥有我的美，你拥有你的艺术，
除此以外，不要重新开始，
这个世界还不够容纳两个人
如你和我。

Wasted Days
(From A Picture Painted by Miss V. T.)

A fair slim boy not made for this world's pain,
With hair of gold thick clustering round his ears,
And longing eyes half veil'd by foolish tears
Like bluest water seen through mists of rain;
Pale cheeks whereon no kiss hath left its stain,
Red under - lip drawn in for fear of Love,
And white throat whiter than the breast of dove—
Alas! alas! if all should be in vain.

Corn - fields behind, and reapers all a - row
In weariest labour toiling wearily,
To no sweet sound of laughter, or of lute;
And careless of the crimson sunset - glow
The boy still dreams: nor knows that night is nigh,
And in the night - time no man gathers fruit.

浪费时光

（来自 V. T. 小姐的一幅画）

画一个英俊且修长的男孩不是来忍受世间的痛苦，
他的耳边留着浓密的金发，
迷惘的泪水遮掩了一半他那热切的双眼
就像透过雨雾看见的那片湛蓝的海水；
苍白的脸颊上没有留下一丝亲吻过的瑕疵，
对爱的畏怯令他收敛起红润的下唇，
白皙的颈部比鸽子的胸脯还要白——
哎呀！哎呀！这一切是否都是徒劳事。

后面是玉米田，收割的人排成一行
农夫们寒耕热耘，早已筋疲力尽，
没有开心甜蜜的笑声，没有琴韵悠扬；
没有人去留意绯红色的落日余晖，
男孩仍然做着白日梦：岂知夜晚已来临，
没有人会在黑夜来把果实采摘。

Thomas Hardy
托马斯·哈代

托马斯·哈代（Thomas Hardy，1840—1928）是英国19世纪后半叶和20世纪初叶最杰出的小说家和诗人之一。哈代的主要成就是在小说方面，如《卡斯特桥市长》（*The Mayor of Casterbridge*，1886）、《德伯家的苔丝》（*Tess of The D'Urbervilles*，1891）和《无名的裘德》（*Jude the Obscure*，1895）等是广为流传的小说。除小说创作，哈代也称得上是所处时代伟大的诗人之一。哈代出版第一部诗集《维塞克斯诗集》（*Wessex Poems and other Verses*，1898）时已是五十八岁，这时他才把主要精力转向诗歌；他一生创作了一千多首短诗和一部长篇史诗《列王》（*Dynasts*，1904）。哈代的诗歌深受华兹华斯（William Wordsworth）的影响，他的抒情诗歌大多短小精干、音乐性极强、描写细腻，纯朴的语言处处闪耀着人性的光辉和深刻的哲理。

An August Midnight

I

A shaded lamp and a waving blind,
And the beat of a clock from a distant floor:
On this scene enter—winged, horned, and spined—
A longlegs, a moth, and a dumbledore;
While 'mid my page there idly stands
A sleepy fly, that rubs its hands…

II

Thus meet we five, in this still place,
At this point of time, at this point in space.
My guests parade my new-penned ink,
Or bang at the lamp-glass, whirl, and sink.
"God's humblest, they!" I muse. Yet why?
They know Earth-secrets that know not I.

八月的一个午夜

一

一盏有灯罩的灯，一幅飘动的百叶窗，
从远处楼层传来时钟的敲打声：
此番场景下登场了：长翅膀的，头上长角的，有脊柱的，
一只长脚蜘蛛，一只飞蛾，一只大黄蜂；
在我的纸页中央还逍遥地站立了
一只昏昏欲睡的苍蝇，正搓着它的手……

二

我们五个相遇在这个静谧的地方，
在这个时间点上，在这个空间点上。
我的访客们在我刚写就的字行上招摇而行，
或撞在灯的玻璃上，旋几个圈，掉落在地面。
“它们是上帝最轻贱的造物！”我沉思道，这是为何？
它们能洞悉大地的秘密，我却全然不知。

I Said to Love

I said to Love,
"It is not now as in old days
When men adored thee and thy ways
All else above;
Named thee the Boy, the Bright, the One
Who spread a heaven beneath the sun,"
I said to Love.

I said to him,
"We now know more of thee than then;
We were but weak in judgment when,
With hearts abrim,
We clamoured thee that thou would'st please
Inflict on us thine agonies,"
I said to him.

I said to Love,
"Thou art not young, thou art not fair,
No faery darts, no cherub air,
Nor swan, nor dove
Are thine; but features pitiless,
And iron daggers of distress,"
I said to Love.

我对爱说

我对爱说，
“今日不比往日
男人们仰慕你和你的仪态
胜于爱其他一切；
把你称作人子、光明、唯一的，
因你在阳光下铺就了天堂，”
我对爱说。

我对他说，
“现在对你的了解远胜于从前；
虽说我们的判断力减弱了，
但内心充盈，
我们大声疾呼请你不要
让你的痛苦来把我们折磨，”
我对他说。

我对爱说，
“你不再年轻，不再漂亮，
没有了仙子的箭，没有了天使的风采，
你不是天鹅，也不再是鸽子
只有令人毫无吝惜的身形，
只有痛苦如铁匕首穿心，”
我对爱说。

"Depart then, Love! ...
—Man's race shall end, dost threaten thou?
The age to come the man of now
Know nothing of? —
We fear not such a threat from thee;
We are too old in apathy!
Mankind shall cease. —So let it be,"
I said to Love.

“我的爱人，出发吧！……
——人类的竞技快结束了，还会威胁你？
如今已步入晚年
却不为你所知？——
我们并不惧怕来自你的恐吓，
我们已年迈体弱无动于衷了！
人类将终结——那就让它来临吧，”
我对爱说。

The Last Leaf

"The leaves throng thick above: —
Well, I'll come back, dear Love,
When they all are down!"
She watched that August tree,

(None now scorned summer as she),
Till it broidered it brown.

And then October came blowing,
And the leaves showed signs they were going,
And she saw up through them.

O how she counted them then!
—November left her but ten,
—And started to strew them.

"Ah, when they all are gone,
And the skeleton – time comes on,
Whom shall I see!"

—When the fifteenth spread its sky
That month, her upturned eye
Could count but three.

And at the close of the week
A flush flapped over her cheek:

最后一片树叶

"树上枝繁叶茂：——
嗯，亲爱的，我会回来的，
当树叶全部掉落时！"
八月时她注视那棵树，

(无人像她那样鄙视夏天)，
直到树叶变成棕色。

十月来时大风吹，
树叶看似要离去，
她抬头仔细望着树叶。

哦，她居然把树叶细数了一遍！
——十一月只留下了十片树叶，
——树叶开始洒满地。

"啊，当树叶全消失，
光秃秃的日子就来了，
我还能瞧见谁！"

——那月十五日天空舒展开来
她抬眼望去，
只数出了三片叶子。

那一周结束时
一片红霞飞上她脸颊：

The last one fell.

But—he did not come. And, at length,
Her hope of him lost all strength,
And it was as a knell...

When he did come again,
Years later, a husband then,
Heavy somewhat,

With a smile she reminded him:
And he cried: "Ah, that vow of our whim!" —
Which I forgot,

"As one does! —And was that the tree?
So it was! —Dear me, dear me:
Yes: I forgot."

最后一片树叶飘落而下。

但是——依然不见他到来。
她对他抱有的希望终成了泡影，
仿佛丧钟已敲响……

他再次回来时，
已是几年过后，他已为人夫，
带着几分悲哀，

她微笑着提醒他：
他却大喊："啊，那是心血来潮的盟誓！"——
我早已不记得了，

"你竟然这样做了——正是那棵树？
原来如此啊！——天啊，天啊：
哦：我居然全忘了。"